SHARING
THE
VICTORY

SHARING
THE
VICTORY

THE TWENTY-FIVE YEARS OF
THE FELLOWSHIP OF CHRISTIAN ATHLETES
BY JOSEPH DUNN
FOREWORD BY TOM LANDRY

quick fox

New York • London • Tokyo

International Standard Book Number: 0-8256-3146-7
Library of Congress Catalog Card Number: 80-50025

In Great Britain: Book Sales Ltd., 78 Newman Street, London W1P 3LA.
In Canada: Gage Trade Publishing, P.O. Box 5000, 164 Commander Blvd.,
Agincourt, Ontario M1S 3C7.
In Japan: Quick Fox, 4-26-22 Jingumae, Shibuya-ku, Tokyo 150.

Design: Barry L.S. Mirenburg
Assistant: David M. Nehila

CONTENTS

FOREWORD

In the 1950s, during my career with the New York Giants, I was searching for meaning in my life. Our team had just competed in the championship game against the Baltimore Colts in one of the greatest games ever played, but I sensed something was still missing. During the off-season a friend invited me to attend a Bible study group that met every Wednesday morning at a local hotel. I was reluctant to go, but finally did, and subsequently accepted Jesus Christ as my Savior.

In 1962 I was invited to attend a Fellowship of Christian Athletes' national conference at Estes Park, Colorado, where I was amazed to find 700 or so athletes and coaches enjoying a week of "inspiration and perspiration." From this experience I knew the FCA movement was an excellent opportunity for me to share my faith with young athletes who, in turn, could influence other young people with the challenge of following Jesus Christ.

My involvement with FCA has given me many opportunities to grow and mature as a Christian. I've had the privilege of knowing most of the men mentioned in this book, and the fellowship of these men has enriched and inspired my life.

One of my FCA highlights was a "Weekend of Champions" in Dallas in 1969. Some 160 athletes and coaches participated in this 3-day event, speaking at high school assemblies, prisons, churches, and business groups. More than 100,000 people heard the Gospel and the FCA story.

In recent years, the "open mike" sharing during the final assembly at national conferences has been one of my most moving FCA experiences. Any of the athletes may come to the platform and express to the group what the week has meant to him. I remember one evening when a young black approached the mike and said, "This week is the first time anyone ever told me they loved me."

During the mid-1960s, the Fellowship invited me to become a member of its National Board of Trustees and I served until the mid-1970s. I spent several years as chairman of the board and I was privileged to be a part of many important decisions that expanded FCA's ministry. The Huddle and Fellowship programs for high school and college boys, the National Resource Center, and official recognition of junior high and female groups were initiated during this decade.

I believe the future of the United States rests in the moral character of its people and that character must be developed in our young people. Outside of the home and church, FCA does this better than any organization I know. Our children face the greatest temptations of any generation in modern times. One of the strongest peer groups in junior and senior high schools is the members of the athletic teams, and FCA seeks to develop Christian leadership in this crucial area of influence.

As a reader you'll have the opportunity not only of enjoying the story of FCA in the following pages, but of "sharing the victory" with those committed people who have made FCA a vital force in our country. My hope is that you will become interested in FCA to the extent that you'll become involved and share the victory, too.

— Tom Landry
Head Coach, Dallas Cowboys Football Team

91
92
155
158
142

A SPECIAL THANKS

To the Fellowship of Christian Athletes we give sincere thanks for its endorsement of this project and for its full cooperation and assistance in supplying the information and the pictures that are contained in these pages.

Skip Stogsdill, a member of the FCA staff and the editor of their magazine, *The Christian Athlete*, opened his files and gave of his energies in tracking down many of the principals in this story. In the latter stages of putting this work together, his encouragement and his enthusiasm became the major ingredients in whatever success this history may enjoy.

The men who labored in the early years, particularly Don McClanen, whose dream became the Fellowship of Christian Athletes, deserve the largest measure of credit for the message contained in these pages. Across the nation, from dining rooms and dens, from business offices and pastor's studies, these men probed their memories of

25 years ago to bring to life the story of how it all began.

And to the legions of men and women whose names do not appear in this history, special recognition is due. Because of lost or misplaced records, or because time simply ran out for the publication of this book, many people are not named in this story. It is hoped that these FCA disciples will take full pride in sharing this part of the Fellowship's victory, even though they have not been specifically mentioned in the book.

A lasting acknowledgment is tended to all of the people within the ranks of the Fellowship of Christian Athletes, past and present, who talked with us, worked with us, and shared very personal feelings with us. We are richer for having met, however briefly, fine people and extraordinary Christians.

— Joseph Dunn

SHARING THE VICTORY

THE
DREAM

The white Pontiac droned along the highway in the direction of Bartlesville, Oklahoma, and toward a man named William Doenges, who owned a Ford automobile agency in that town. The year was 1954.

Behind the wheel, sometimes concentrating on the road but more often focusing his mind on the mission of the long drive, was Don McClanen, 29-year-old basketball coach, athletic director, and general helpmate for all athletic programs at the small college called Eastern Oklahoma A & M.

Beside him was his wife, Gloria, silently turning over in her mind the reason for the trip and the deep tie to her husband that bound her almost inexplicably to the journey and its uncertain ending.

In the back seat were their two children, Michael, 5, and Judy, 4, for the most part unaware, as children are, of anything save the seldom-changing scene of the Oklahoma flatland.

Don glanced up from the road ahead to the rear-view mirror. Behind him stretched mile after mile of roadway leading back to Wilburton, Oklahoma, where he and Gloria had a modest home on the campus, and where he had a coaching career that was beginning to blossom. Behind him also lay 7 years of nurturing a dream.

His handsome face, for most of the drive serious, broke into a gentle, thoughtful smile as he remembered the mileposts in his life and in Gloria's since the loss of their first child, since he had given his life and his endeavors into the hands of the Lord.

His eyes returned to the road, and, as he had done since a day alone in a church in Oklahoma City when he had surrendered his will to God, Don McClanen looked ahead with quiet confidence. He was not far away from Bartlesville and a man who was to help him change untold thousands of lives.

The previous 7 years had tested Don and Gloria McClanen.

He had become, during those 7 years, closely and yet sometimes only vaguely aware that God was leading him. He was comforted in that knowledge. But the two McClanens had paid a price for that comfort, a price in pain and in disappointment.

Don left the submarine service after World War II, married Gloria, his high-school sweetheart, and moved from his native Pennsylvania to Stillwater, where he had enrolled under the GI bill at Oklahoma A & M College, now Oklahoma State University. He wanted to play football, but it didn't take much time to learn that he wasn't good enough for A & M's brand of play. He was cut from the squad.

He became impressed with Hank Iba, then head basketball coach of the 1945 and 1946 national-champion A & M basketball team and also A & M's athletic director. Don became manager of the varsity basketball team and decided to become a coach.

But Don McClanen, dedicated to a coaching career, wasn't much aware of the national athletic scene in the year 1947.

It was the year that Joe Fulks led Philadelphia to the NBA championship with 1,389 points, an average of 23.2 a game.

That year, Jet Pilot won the Kentucky Derby, Phalanx the Belmont Stakes, and Faultless the Preakness, splitting the Triple Crown three ways. The Chicago Cardinals beat the Philadelphia Eagles, 28–21, for the NFL championship.

The New York Yankees took the Brooklyn Dodgers 4 games to 3 in the World Series, the Yankees' Joe DiMaggio was the American League MVP and Bob Elliott of Boston was the winner in the National League, while Ted Williams of the Boston Red Sox was the Triple Crown winner, leading at the plate during the season in batting, runs batted in, and home runs.

Illinois outclassed UCLA in the granddaddy of them all, the Rose Bowl, 45–14. And off Santa Cruz Island, a man named C. W. Stewart hooked and boated a still-world-record sailfish for the Pacific Coast. The fish weighed in at 221 pounds and it measured 10', 9" in length.

More enduring achievements in the world of athletics had begun that year in a hospital room near the Stillwater campus, however. Gloria McClanen rested in bed. Her husband sat beside her. And Larry Shonfelt, the associate pastor of First Presbyterian Church in Stillwater and pastor of the Westminster Foundation at the college, was also in the room.

At the foot of Gloria's bed was a small casket that held the couple's 2-day-old son. Grief had been dulled by a deep love and a faith, still unrefined, in Don McClanen. As the three shared the quiet of the room, he softly offered a brief prayer. "Thy will be done." Larry Shonfelt was moved and he fixed his eyes and mind on the quiet, unassuming young man whose young faith was being tested.

Don McClanen that day began to think deeply and seriously about his beliefs. And he was still thinking of his relationship to God 3 months later when Reverend Shonfelt asked him to prepare a 3-minute talk, as part of a panel discussion during a Sunday night service in the First Presbyterian Church, entitled "Making My Vocation Christian."

The sophomore student who had seen service aboard a submarine and who was now planning to coach young men confronted a real challenge. He began to analyze how a coach could use his talents to encourage, in himself and in those he touched, a life for Christ. When he entered the room in church that night with several other students, he had the germ of an idea. He knew that young people, particularly those in junior high and high school, looked up to recognized athletes on the college level, and that the college athletes looked with respect to the men in the professional ranks. Somehow, he thought, there must be a way to turn that sense of awe and hero-worship into a positive force for the church and for Christ.

As he gave his 3-minute talk on the panel with a home economics student, an architectural student, and an engineering student, he wasn't sure how his idea might be put into practice. And he wasn't really conscious that God was beginning to lead him along a path that would deepen his faith and make him an instrument for good in the lives of young men and young women throughout the country. Don McClanen, however, had the embryo of an idea, clothed in a question: How do you relate Christ to the athletic world and how do you relate the athletic world to Christ?

Shortly after his talk, he began a practice that,

strangely, had no immediate value for him: As he would thumb through magazines and newspapers at home and in his small office, he would clip out the occasional article about a well-known athlete who was speaking in terms of his own commitment to Christ.

One such clipping came from *Life* magazine. It was a picture of a man named Dr. Louis H. Evans, Sr. The caption identified Evans as a former great athlete and one of the 10 outstanding clergymen in the country. The words under the picture of the imposing man told how Dr. Evans made use of athletic jargon in his sermons and some of his prayers. Another that caught Don's eye was a story on Otto Graham, then quarterback for the Cleveland Browns, which appeared in a small magazine called *Guideposts*, an inspirational monthly for all faiths. And there was one on Branch Rickey, then general manager of the Pittsburgh Pirates.

The top drawer in Don's bureau in their bedroom became the repository for the occasional clippings he found. Cutting them out and saving them became a ritual with some vague purpose unstated, much like the housewife carefully tucking away coupons and trading stamps for an undefined article sometime in the future.

Several months after his 3-minute talk, Don McClanen found himself shifted from the roles of a panel speaker and magazine and newspaper reader to the role of a listener.

The words came from H. Clay Fiske, who had journeyed from his work in the Tulsa school system to Oklahoma City to speak at a conference on physical education. Don was perhaps the most attentive member of the audience. As he listened closely to the older man discuss the worth and inspiration that could come from a coaching career, he felt himself moved and caught up in Fiske's message. There was no mention of religion in the address, but the impact of the speaker's words directed the young coaching student onto the streets of Oklahoma City at noontime along a path alone and away from other conference participants who headed for lunch in small knots of newfound acquaintances.

He walked into the first church that he came to, a Roman Catholic Church, and there, in the back pew, in the serenity that comes often with stillness and solitude, Don McClanen knelt down and surrendered his will to the Lord.

He rose slowly and, with an increased sense of purpose, soon retraced his steps to the conference. He felt no welling of emotion, no sudden glow of rightness in his life, but rather the birth of his understanding that God had taken hold of his life and would, in His own way, direct him.

What he did feel, with a little less vagueness now, was that he might find an answer to his question, the question that had been raised when he prepared for a 3-minute talk: "How to enlist a group of Christians who happened to be athletes and how to have them share God's victory by touching the lives of coaches and athletes of all ages and by strengthening the church."

THE
BEGINNING

Don McClanen's question remained with him. The answer, if there was one, was slow in coming. But the timing was perhaps fortuitous. Don was now heavily involved in classwork and preparation for a coaching career.

Larry Shonfelt had received a call and had left the A & M campus for another church. In his place, both as a pastor and a friend to Don, was Bob Geller.

During the rest of his undergraduate schooling and through his year working for his Master's degree, Don would drop by the Gellers' and talk with Bob about his idea. The response was always encouraging, but neither man at the time knew exactly how to proceed. Yet the topic of coaches' and athletes' impacts on a Christian life was never far from mind when the two got together or when they and their wives shared an evening.

Don was slowly becoming aware that he thought more

and more often about the beauty that existed in the athletic world, despite its connotation of ego, strength, and rule-contained violence—a beauty, cleanness, and purpose that was similar to that which he could see in all other areas of life. But he was more aware on a daily basis of pushing himself through school and locating a coaching job. His GI Bill money and the money that Gloria made as a full-time employee of the telephone company was sufficient to get by on, but he wanted to build a family and a place for that family.

Graduation brought the diploma he expected, but not the kind of coaching job he'd hoped for. He had remained in the Reserves upon his discharge from the submarine service. And the U.S. found itself again involved with war, this time in a place called Korea. Colleges were afraid to hire a veteran who was still in the Reserves.

Through his mentor, Hank Iba, Don was offered a coaching job in a small rural consolidated school system in Norfolk, Oklahoma, just outside Stillwater. Glad at least to be working, Don began to practice what had been preached to him at A & M and what he had learned as a manager to Iba's great teams.

Don had learned well. His team, his very first, won 29 games that year. It lost 2. And that record advanced him the next year to Eastern Oklahoma State in Wilburton, where his pay was $3,600 a year and he and Gloria had a small house on the campus. His jobs were head basketball coach and athletic director; and overseer, assistant, and helper to all of the college's sports. There were two children in the McClanen household now: Michael, born in December 1948, and Judy, born in February 1950.

Don's life was busy. He was doing well as a basketball coach. Twice, Eastern Oklahoma had gone to the national playoffs in its division. It also boasted a state championship. Don was a good coach, he knew it, and the record proved it. It was the pattern of so many coaches who had advanced before him; he sensed that a major college and the making of his mark were part of his future.

Still, he made road trips that didn't end at locker rooms or gymnasiums, but at Bob Geller's driveway. The association that had started when he was a student at A & M had long since become a deep friendship, no matter the intervening miles or months. And the talks now had broadened to family matters, coaching matters, and Christian matters. But his questioning dream of coaches and athletes and their potential for enlarging Christian life always surfaced.

The answer, unexpectedly and without fanfare, surfaced on a page in the *Daily Oklahoman*, delivered one morning in March 1954 to the front door of the McClanen's small home in Wilburton.

Don stopped thumbing through the paper and focused his eyes on an article announcing that Dr. Louis H. Evans, Sr., was scheduled to speak in Oklahoma City, about 150 miles northwest of Wilburton, to a Presbyterian men's meeting. He called to Gloria and showed her the article. He didn't have to leave his chair and go to the now-familiar top drawer in the bedroom. He knew that one of the clippings that he had stored carefully away contained a picture and information on Dr. Evans.

Together, as they approached everything in their lives, Don and Gloria McClanen made plans to go to Oklahoma City. Don had a feeling of excitement and anticipation, as though more parts of the answer to his dream might lie less than 200 miles away. But there was to be a disappointment. Don's first obligation was to his Lord, with his family next. And that meant he should do his job as well as he could. Don had coaching responsibilities on the Thursday night that Evans was to be in Oklahoma City. There was no agonizing over a decision, no discussion with Gloria about which place to be. He knew, and that was that. He missed Dr. Evans. And he wondered, after he

11

Branch Rickey, father of modern-day baseball, and early supporter of FCA.

Don McClanen, the young coach from Oklahoma, whose dream was to become reality.

McClanen at FCA headquarters shortly after it was founded. The blackboard shows a listing of upcoming meetings and speakers for each.

Four of the founding fathers of FCA. (L to R) Dr. Louis Evans, Dr. Roe Johnston, Don McClanen, Branch Rickey.

Dr. Louis Evans, Sr., today.

Athlete-minister, Dr. Roe Johnston.

discovered the scheduling conflict, what might have come out of a meeting with the man. He tried to remain cheerful and put the disappointment aside, but he had been so close to a man who might really be able to give him further guidance, and possibly a new direction to his life—he was, without question, discouraged. He tried to shake the unhappiness as he and Gloria drove on Friday, the day after he would have been in Dr. Evans' presence, to Stillwater and a weekend with the Gellers. But he was unusually introspective and, from time to time during the drive, he grumbled. He pulled the Pontiac into the driveway and had hardly stepped out to walk around to open the door for Gloria when June Geller came out of the house to greet them.

She was glad they had arrived early, explaining that the Gellers were expecting a guest for supper and saying she was happy that Don and Gloria would be able to join them. As they walked into the house, she told them that the dinner guest was Dr. Louis H. Evans. He was in Stillwater for Religious Emphasis Week on the campus of Oklahoma State.

Don McClanen's heart and his spirit jumped. Of all people who could have been there that night, Louis Evans would have been first on his list. The disappointment and the frustration at missing a man suddenly so important to him and to his dream fell away.

That evening, Don poured out his dream to Evans: the idea of a ministry of coaches and athletes, the harnessing of heroes to reach those who idolized them for a life for the Lord, the names in the magazine and newspaper articles that Don still kept in a dresser drawer.

Evans was spontaneous in his enthusiasm. That night the two men prayed about the idea. They talked and prayed again the next morning. Evans saw it as a great idea, but cautioned that they should research the athletic world so as not to duplicate someone else's similar effort.

But Evans poured a strong fertilizing potion on the idea that Don had nursed with Bob Geller's help. He urged Don to write to the men featured in the clippings, and find out if they would be willing to serve in this beginning of a coming-together of a kind of fellowship of Christian athletes.

Don did write to them when he returned to Wilburton and the top dresser drawer became a file cabinet of possible disciples of a dream. There were 19 people and Don wrote each of them, beginning in April:

- Doak Walker, All-Pro halfback of the Detroit Lions
- Carl Erskine, veteran pitcher for the Brooklyn Dodgers
- Otto Graham, quarterback for the Cleveland Browns
- Reverend Bob Richards, Olympic gold-medal pole-vaulter
- R. J. Robinson, All-American basketball player at Baylor
- Donn Moomaw, All-American linebacker at UCLA
- Bob Mathias, Olympic decathlon gold medalist
- Alvin Dark, shortstop for the Boston Braves
- Dean Cromwell, famed track coach at USC
- Bud Wilkinson, head football coach, University of Oklahoma
- Glenn Cunningham, Olympics competitor and world-champion miler from Kansas
- Dan Towler, All-Pro running back for the Los Angeles Rams
- Biggie Munn, head football coach, Michigan State
- Roe Johnston, All-American end at the Naval Academy
- Red Barber, former sportscaster for the Brooklyn Dodgers
- Tom Harmon, All-American halfback and Heisman Trophy winner at the University of Michigan

- Alonzo Stagg, football coach at University of Chicago and College of Pacific
- Louie Sanporenie, Olympic track star
- Branch Rickey, general manager of the Pittsburgh Pirates.

In his letters to these men, Don stated his belief that America was a hero-worshipping society, that many of the country's youth wouldn't listen to their parents or take their pastors seriously about the positive side of Christian life. He went on in his letters to explain that he felt most of America's young would listen to the men who competed on athletic fields; and that those he wanted to enlist in his army were the people who weren't afraid to acknowledge their faith. Don also stated that none of the men would be paid or receive financial gain in return for his help.

As he waited to see whether any of these giants in the world of American sports would send a message back to him in his small corner of southeast Oklahoma, Don McClanen now knew that God was leading him. If he needed evidence, it came in 14 envelopes from the 19 athletes to whom he had written, a remarkable response that strengthened Don's resolve. Most of the letters were brief, one or two paragraphs. But each said yes, he would be willing to give his time and his service.

Don wondered what the commitment to service would mean to these men. But the wondering and the thinking had to take a back seat to action now. And the action Don was to take would bring a tension as yet unknown to him and to Gloria.

He felt he had to speak with some of the 14 letter-writers personally, to insure that they were willing to do the kind of work that he envisioned. But he had no money for travel and all of the athletes were far distant from Oklahoma. He talked with Gloria, who was his comrade and his confidante as well as his wife. They prayed.

Don believed that his wife shared in his course of action

as he approached a banker in Wilburton who respected the coaching job that Don was doing at Eastern Oklahoma. The banker was sympathetic; Don left the bank with $1,000. The family car had been put up as collateral on a mortgage. When he got home and told Gloria that he had mortgaged the car for the $1,000 needed to visit some of the athletes, Don found that Gloria's reaction was not what he had expected. Gloria was his supporter and wanted him to pursue this goal, but not at the expense of the family and its needs.

The two of them were suddenly in the maelstrom of a financial argument that cut to the heart of their marriage. Don had misread her commitment to his dream. In following his dream, he had been blind to her needs and her hopes and fears as a wife and a mother. The days and the evenings were filled with tension and discord in the McClanen home. But in the end, as in the beginning of their relationship, they were of one mind and a single purpose. Don McClanen went to see some of the athletes in order to plumb the depth of their intent. And he went with Gloria's blessing. He returned uplifted by the visits, but with work still to do and no money with which to do it.

It was now May 1954. Don heard from G. Raymond Campbell, a Presbyterian pastor in Oklahoma City. Campbell had talked to Don earlier about being a youth coordinator for the church and Don at that time had spoken in general terms of his idea. The minister had told him that when the time was right and the need was apparent the Christian Laymen's League of Oklahoma City would try to help with some money for the effort. Ray Campbell soon delivered $1,000 to Don; enough money for Don to further explore his idea with more people who might share in the effort. God truly had his hand in the effort, Don thought.

One person Don visited was Leonard E. LeSourd, the managing editor of *Guideposts*, the inspirational

Quarterback Otto Graham explaining the proper handoff technique at an early FCA gathering.

Business executive Paul Benedum.

Leonard LeSourd.

The Rev. Gary Demarest who took on the role of emcee in the early
days of the FCA Conferences.

19

magazine that had carried the story on Otto Graham. LeSourd was in *Guideposts'* New York editorial offices on East 46th Street when he was told that a young man was waiting to speak to him. The young man introduced himself as Don McClanen, a coach at a small Oklahoma college, who then launched into his idea for a new kind of sports organization.

LeSourd listened with growing interest. McClanen talked about a fellowship of Christian athletes and coaches and the impact they could have in bringing Christ to hero-worshipping youngsters. He explained to LeSourd that he had read of such athletes in *Guideposts* and was trying to contact as many of them as he could. Branch Rickey's name was mentioned. LeSourd's father had played baseball under the careful coaching eye of Rickey at Ohio Wesleyan and Rickey was a family friend of LeSourd's.

The word "fellowship" began to take on a living meaning. Before Don left, Leonard LeSourd had provided *Guideposts* articles by 7 men in the athletic spotlight including Rickey, his friendship, and a timely gift of inspiration, belief in the dream, and encouragement.

Don's next call was at the offices of the National Council of Churches, where he met with James L. Stoner, at the time director of the University Christian Mission. Jim Stoner wanted to know how much emphasis would be put on the athletes in the college ranks. Don said that the college campus would be the major focus of his efforts. Stoner expressed an interest in the possibility of the program. In calling on Stoner, Don had touched an area vital to his idea: the church.

But successes in New York were countered by failure in Pittsburgh, where Branch Rickey was located. Rickey had been one of the original 19 men to whom Don had written without receiving a reply. Talking with Rickey grew to a near-obsession with Don. He had read about the man and his good works in baseball, his Christian attitude, and his belief that men of character and worth were men who should wear his uniform. But getting to see him proved a difficult task.

Don resorted to telephone calls to Rickey's offices in Pittsburgh, where he was executive vice-president and general manager of the Pirates. First Ken Blackburn, Rickey's secretary, discouraged Don. Undaunted, Don got through to Branch Rickey, Jr., only to be rebuffed again. Dad's health is not very good and he's under tremendous pressure right now, the son told Don. Don had run into a natural and expected shield guarding Rickey, who had spent time in Saranac Lake, N. Y., in 1907 when tuberculosis ended his baseball playing career.

But Don McClanen persisted. He felt that Rickey would support his idea if it were explained to him. And Don wanted and needed the kind of support that a man of Rickey's standing in the athletic world could lend to the idea.

Don had to travel from Oklahoma to Pennsylvania with his family in August, and he called Rickey's office again before starting the long drive. He asked if he could have 5 minutes with Rickey if he could get to his Pittsburgh office. He promised not to bother anyone in the Pirates' organization again if he was given the 5-minute meeting. Don put his family up in a Pittsburgh motel on a Monday night and was in Rickey's outer office as soon as it opened the next day. Rickey came in shortly after Don took a seat, and within 10 minutes summoned Don into his office. The hoped-for 5-minute meeting turned into 5 hours of serious and probing conversation.

Rickey understood Don's idea quickly, but he wanted details. And he spent much of the 5 hours challenging the conviction that Don McClanen had about this idea of a fellowship of Christian athletes. He wanted to assure himself that the young coach from Oklahoma was a deeply

21

committed Christian and not simply another sports fan who was interested in another program on physical culture for athletes. The 7 years of maturing in the service of the Lord while his dream also matured into an idea served Don McClanen well.

Rickey's understanding of the idea became a belief in the idea. But he was troubled about Don's ability to continue coaching and also pursue the dream. He told Don that he would need at least $10,000. Rickey's business mind had analyzed Don's situation: family obligations, coaching job, no time to implement the idea. He was afraid that Don would overwork himself in trying to meet his personal obligations and at the same time trying to begin the movement.

He again told Don that $10,000 was needed. As he looked at Don, he scratched the thick eyebrows that were one of his hallmarks. He thought reflectively, moving his cigar in and then out of his mouth. Finally, he said, "I think I may know the man who would be willing to give that $10,000."

Branch Rickey, the man who was called the Father of Modern Baseball, who had implemented the idea of the farm club, who had made baseball a respectable sport and brought females to the parks with the idea of Ladies' Day, the man who broke the race barrier with Jackie Robinson, in that meeting with Don signed on with McClanen and his idea of a fellowship of Christian athletes. Rickey promised to play an active role in the movement. He wasted no time in living up to that promise.

THE
FELLOWSHIP

It was a Branch Rickey challenge that had put the white Pontiac, Don McClanen, and his family on the road to Bartlesville, Oklahoma, that day in 1954. "If you can get some of the athletes to Pittsburgh, I think I can get you that $10,000 and some additional help," Rickey had told Don.

But again the McClanen bank account was hovering near a zero balance. Don's car remained mortgaged for $1,000, debts were mounting for his travels and contacts, and now he needed $900 to fly several of the athletes East to meet with Rickey. He desperately needed help.

Bill Doenges ran a successful Ford agency in Bartlesville, Oklahoma, and also managed to travel the state as a Methodist Conference lay leader. He had been an athlete, too. During the Depression era, he had quarterbacked Lynn O. Waldorf's Oklahoma City University football team. And although he liked football more than other

23

sports, he had been a better basketball player. He competed on the tennis, track, and wrestling teams, but football remained his first love. It was a wide-open brand of football in those days, too, no signals from the bench, passes on fourth downs, quick kicks. Real excitement.

But Doenges now found his excitement and reward in church activity. He was even helping to provide transportation for Oklahoma University football players so that they could visit nearby churches and talk with young people on weekends. Bill Doenges, like Don McClanen, believed that athletes could make a contribution to a greater Christian life and he was interested in Don's program, although he knew few details.

Don had called Doenges. The two had never met. In the telephone conversation, Don only said that he was trying to start a movement with Christian athletes and that he would like to talk. In addition, Don knew that he needed $2,000 to clear his debts and get a group of athletes to Pittsburgh. He wanted to talk to Doenges about money, but he wanted a face-to-face meeting.

Thus, McClanen took the road to Bartlesville, accompanied by his family. The Pontiac pulled up outside the Doenges Ford agency and Don headed inside. As they waited in the car, Gloria and the two McClanen children offered their prayers for a successful meeting. When Don reappeared, he had a check for $2,200, a new friend and supporter in Bill Doenges, and the means to gather athletes in Pittsburgh and also to pay off the $1,000 on his car.

Branch Rickey had persuaded several influential and wealthy Pittsburgh businessmen to listen to the story that Don and the athletes wanted to tell.

Don McClanen, a small-college basketball coach with a large and growing idea, got off a plane in Pittsburgh. So did several athletes whose names were known throughout the nation. So did Bill Doenges, the automobile dealer

24

from Bartlesville, whose $2,200 turned the modest beginning of a fellowship into a movement with nationwide potential for the Lord.

Some of the visitors who stayed in the YMCA as guests of Branch Rickey formed the first advisory board for Don's idea. And out of that group of men and that first advisory board came living examples of man's commitment to Christ, as they rolled up their sleeves and hammered out a proposed constitution and plan of operation.

After the advisory board had been formed and had met, there was another meeting in Pittsburgh. It was with a small group of Pittsburgh businessmen. Dr. Evans shared with the business and professional leaders of Pittsburgh his belief in Don's dream. He told them that the idea would mean a great change for the better in the lives of athletes, coaches, and all whom they influenced. He pointed to some of the athletes in attendance and told the businessmen: "These men have the muscle to make this work; you have the money. We need to get the two together."

Among the men at that meeting was Pittsburgh industrialist Paul G. Benedum. A close friend of Rickey's, Benedum had arranged the meeting and had called some of his business friends together. Benedum had been graduated from Ohio State University in 1927 and had begun work that year as a geologist and district manager of the Benedum-Trees Oil Company. He went on to found 1 oil company and to serve as president of 3 others. He was recognized for his contributions to community endeavors as much as for his success in business, and particularly for his contributions to young Americans through gifts and assistance to educational institutions.

With nothing more to go on than the outline of one man's dream and the enthusiasm of 3 people at the meeting — Branch Rickey, Louis Evans, and Don McClanen — Paul Benedum gave $10,000 of his own money to the idea. And

Olympic pole vault champion Bob Richards clearing the bar in a drizzling rain with only auto headlights for illumination.

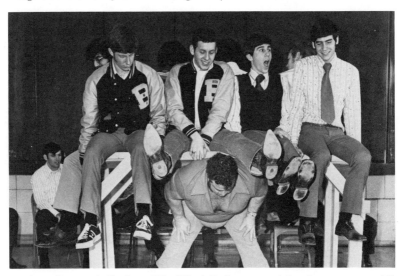

Paul Anderson, billed as "The World's Strongest Man," prepares to lift some young athletes in 1972.

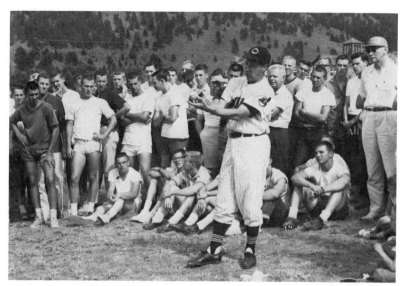

Bob Feller demonstrating how to hold a fast ball.

NBA great Bob Pettit offers pointers at 1962 National Conference.

with that $10,000, the idea became a truly national movement even before it had even become a local movement in Oklahoma. Paul G. Benedum added Don McClanen's movement to the list of organizations and institutions in which he believed.

Benedum, a wise businessman, had listened carefully to the men and had watched their faces. He had been immediately impressed that Branch Rickey was part of the effort. He had been impressed that Dr. Evans, who had spent 10 years of his ministry in Pittsburgh and who was well known to Benedum, was strong in his belief.

After that meeting, which turned into a celebration sharing an important victory, Paul Benedum said to Rickey that the fellowship was the most exciting idea he'd ever heard of. It was so natural, so down to earth. He believed it was bound to have an unending effect on the youth across the nation.

With the gift of $10,000, the 3 founders of the movement were in a position to spread the word. And with them was a fourth man who earlier had listened to Don's dream and had expressed his belief in its worth. That man was Roe Johnston, an All-American end at the United States Naval Academy.

Johnston had been one of the first people in the athletic world whom Don McClanen had talked with face to face. Johnston was in the Presbyterian ministry in Indianapolis and Don had focused on him because of his athletic background and because Bob Geller had suggested that Johnston, as a minister, might have important insights to add to the idea.

Johnston, like the other 3, knew that money was a necessary ingredient to go with the commitment and the deep belief of the small band of early supporters. And he, like the rest, left Pittsburgh with a goal of reaching the athletic arena for Christ and locating the necessary leadership and money to get the job done.

The meaning of the word "fellowship" was now being lived by a slowly increasing number of men who had committed themselves to witnessing to their Christian life in a unique way. It was a fellowship rooted and nursed by their spirit far more than by their physical association. Letters criss-crossed the country. Telephone lines carried the message of a fellowship of Christian athletes to the four points of the compass. Don continued to collect names, names that were suggested by the early participants and names that were volunteered by others who wanted to become a part of God's work through coaches and athletes.

Close to home, Don McClanen began to build. He managed to get Otto Graham and Doak Walker to come to the University of Oklahoma, where they visited with freshmen and varsity football players.

Jim Rodgers was the minister to University of Oklahoma students at the time of the visit and he was disheartened because he felt that the meeting started off so slowly. He had joined a small group of OU athletes to hear Walker, one of the great athletes of college and pro football, give his Christian witness. Rodgers had fostered great hopes for the meeting, but he felt it had been stillborn and now nobody there knew quite how to get the group on the right track. Walker finally came to a stop and everyone sat around feeling embarrassed and looking at the floor.

Rodgers remembers Walker asking, "Does anyone have any questions?" The silence that always follows such a question invaded the room and everyone shuffled, but no one raised a hand.

Finally, just to fill the awkward silence, someone asked Walker, "Last week I watched you on television and I noticed that when a fight broke out on the field, you went over to the sidelines and stood with your head bowed. Were you praying?"

There was a pause while Walker fidgeted. Finally he

looked the speaker in the eye and blurted, "To tell you the truth, no. I wasn't praying. I weigh 187 pounds and that opposing line averaged something like 245. I thought it was safer to go and stand on the sidelines."

Walker's candidness cut through the strained atmosphere and suddenly the meeting became real to the students. They relaxed and opened up. And so did the speakers. It was as though Doak Walker's honesty had given the small group of OU athletes permission to talk about a real faith. And the athletes did talk about faith, their faith. They became interested in what Doak Walker was saying and in the organization that he spoke for.

Two of the freshmen who were at OU when Graham and Walker came were Bill Krisher and Clendon Thomas. They listened as these athletes shared their Christian beliefs and their hope for an organization to carry out the work of God. Their response was, "If Otto and Doak can come here, we can go, as Christians, to the locker rooms and assembly halls of every high school in this state." And that's what they set out to do.

Away from home, when his time and the precious funds allowed, Don also began to build. He waited one summer afternoon in the lobby of the Warwick Hotel in Philadelphia during the 1954 baseball season. He wanted to talk to Carl Erskine. Erskine had had his best season the year before, winning 20 games and losing only 6. The All-Star pitcher was the topic of baseball talk and commercial offers. The Dodgers were in town for a series with the Phillies when Erskine was met in the lobby by the small and unpretentious man who introduced himself as Don McClanen.

Don outlined in detail the idea of a fellowship of Christian athletes, following up his letter. Erskine was led to feel that he should help. He told Don to count him in, although neither of them could define what such a commitment might mean.

As Don McClanen went about collecting the athletes whose names and witness were needed for the fellowship, Roe Johnston continued on another part of the mission: seeking funds to add to the Doenges and Benedum startup gifts that had launched the movement.

Johnston had heard about a man named J. Irwin Miller, who headed the Irwin-Sweeney-Miller Foundation. That was all Johnston knew and all that he needed to know at that time.

Four years out of the seminary, young and brash, Roe Johnston picked up the phone in his study one morning and called Miller. He was taken aback when he got directly through to the industrialist, but he quickly gained his composure and explained who he was and that he had an idea that might appeal to Miller. He said he planned to be in Columbus, Ohio, about 2:30 that afternoon and would like to stop by. Even more surprising to Johnston, Miller told him to come ahead.

When Johnston was ushered into Miller's presence, he launched immediately into an explanation of the McClanen dream and after a few minutes he had summed up the idea and suggested that Miller might want to contribute to the movement.

Miller pressed a buzzer on his desk and Richard B. Stoner, who oversaw the expenditure of the Foundation's funds, came into the office. Johnston repeated his story. At the conclusion, Miller turned to Stoner and asked him to meet with this group and find out more about them.

With Don McClanen and his small army of athletes fanning out across the nations' towns and cities and playing fields, the fellowship began to take concrete form. On the twelfth day of November 1954, at Norman, Oklahoma, the first set of bylaws for the organization was approved and the State of Oklahoma issued a charter to an organization named Fellowship of Christian Athletes.

Pain and pride are attendant to birth; and Don

McClanen would look back at the heartache of deep family discord over money, at the struggle of his own immature Christian life in the process of growth, at the pain of wondering and waiting for an answer to the meaning of an important chapter of his life. But he also could find a sense of inner pride at being led by God's hand to see through the laying down of the firm foundation of a Christian dream.

But most of all, Don McClanen perhaps could see now that much more work was needed in order for thousands of people to share the victory that God had given through Jesus Christ.

Don McClanen kept his sleeves rolled up. When he could find time from coaching, he laid out a plan to take his idea to the public. With still only a handful of athletes committed to lend their time and perhaps their witness in public, he selected Tulsa, Oklahoma City, and Stillwater as sites for trial rallies. The rallies would be the real "Kickoff for the FCA." It was January 1955, two months after the charter had been received.

Don made another trip to the bank in order to borrow again on the faithful family car. He left armed with another borrowed $1,000. He also had in his arsenal the promised appearances of sport stars Otto Graham, Doak Walker, Carl Erskine, Pepper Martin, Reverend Bob Richards, and Baylor basketball All-American Jack Robinson. There were two new names: Dr. Glen Olds, the Methodist chaplain at the University of Denver and a former boxer, and Bob Fenimore, All-American football player at Oklahoma State. Don McClanen was able to smile with a knowledge that his idea was going to touch a lot of lives. And it did. Eighteen thousand citizens—young men and women and parents, athletes and non-athletes—in the three cities turned out to meet the great athletes of the day. It was the biggest turnout thus far for the infant organization.

McClanen was away from Wilburton as often as possible now. There was a second meeting of the advisory board in Pittsburgh. Rickey again was host. The meeting was called to check the progress of the organization and to bring the interested businessmen up to date. The men left more excited than at the first meeting as they heard of the successful kickoff and crowds in Oklahoma.

Don left Pittsburgh, checked in at home and at the office, and was quickly back on the road. This time it was to the West Coast and the University of Washington in Seattle. He had heard that Gary Demarest, a young clergyman and former baseball pitcher at the University of California, and Donn Moomaw, the former 3-time football All-American at UCLA, who was at the time a seminary student, might be interested. Would they help? The two men answered with a single word: Yes. And from that day on, Gary Demarest, who was making preparations to go to Princeton Seminary that fall for a graduate degree, began to travel whenever he could to wherever the Fellowship was meeting.

McClanen was down in Ft. Worth, Texas, getting ready to meet with an insurance executive named James Jeffrey. Jeffrey had been a running back at Baylor, setting a rushing record there in 1950. Don had obtained his name, as he had other names, from one of the athletes who had joined the cause at the outset, Jack Robinson. Robinson knew Jeffrey to be a man who had deep Christian convictions who would probably want to assist the Fellowship. As Don unfolded the idea to Jeffrey, he could see quickly that the insurance man wanted to help and would help. And so it went through the early part of 1955. It remained difficult for Don. He was trying to really launch the Fellowship, but he also had his coaching job to handle and his family to look after. The pressure on him began easing a little around mid-year; it was June and the demands of the basketball program were not so great. It was a good

NFL star "Deacon" Dan Towler helping young

athletes at demonstration in Ashland, Ore., Conference.

35

thing, too, he thought, because another meeting was scheduled in Pittsburgh.

Paul Benedum, who had supplied the $10,000 to launch Don on his roadtrips for the Fellowship nearly 9 months earlier, had another package of good news waiting for Don and the Fellowship in Pittsburgh. Benedum, through his influence and his friendships in the oil industry, had obtained $10,000 from Gulf Oil to help the Fellowship, money that was sorely needed if the work was to continue. With that additional gift, the organization could now make itself known in ever-widening circles.

Don went home and shared with Gloria the most recent events in Pittsburgh. He then took action that demonstrated his and his wife's commitment to the Fellowship: he resigned his coaching job in Wilburton and opened a small back office in the First National Bank Building in Norman, Oklahoma. Don was now the first full-time executive director of the Fellowship of Christian Athletes.

The $10,000 gift from Gulf Oil was put to use in underwriting the cost of the Fellowship's first film, *More Than Champions*. The movie featured Branch Rickey, Doak Walker, Carl Erskine, Bob Richards, Alvin Dark, Red Barber, and Dr. Evans. The film provided a powerful tool for Don to use in spreading the word to other people.

In addition to the film, there was written material that assisted the Fellowship in telling its story. Don had called on Len LeSourd and *Guideposts* magazine in New York. Len and his associates helped produce a brochure on the Fellowship and the brochure was soon a calling card in countless cities.

Roe Johnston was named the first president of the organization before the end of 1955 and he almost immediately found himself in the middle of the first major test of the young organization. As a result of the brochures being mailed throughout the country, the growing list of name athletes and coaches becoming associated with the

Fellowship, and the effort to contact the nation's sports writers, Roe Johnston received a telephone call and an attractive offer. The offer was from an emcee of a national television show who wanted to put a number of big-name athletes on the show to talk about the Fellowship. He explained to Roe what he had in mind and how such a show would provide national exposure for the Fellowship. During the conversation he alluded to what he called a minor point: the name. He said that the name would have to be changed to something like Fellowship of Religious Athletes as the current name was too limiting in its application for a national television audience.

Johnston foresaw problems. The Fellowship needed publicity in order to gather momentum and gain national stature, but he personally didn't believe that the name ought to be changed. He put it before members of the first board. The question launched more than just a discussion. Meetings were held. Phone calls seemed endless. Tempers sometimes were near flaring. In the end, the decision was made to keep the original name. Dr. Evans put his future participation on the line: if the name was going to be changed, he would withdraw his support.

When the words had died down, Don McClanen and all the others who had participated in the decision knew that the Fellowship of Christian Athletes had passed a crucial test. As a result, the men were aware there was a reservoir of inner strength available when critical judgments had to be made.

Shortly after that decision, Don McClanen received a clipping from a sports column in a major daily newspaper. The columnist only mentioned the Fellowship, but what he said hurt Don and made him wonder about his dream. The columnist expressed surprise and dismay that a person of Branch Rickey's standing in the athletic world would lend his name and his efforts to such an organization. The column went on to predict that such a fellow-

37

ship would set up discord among the athletic world, where there were so many diverse faiths, each one important to its followers.

Don went to Rickey and showed him the clipping. Rickey, never showing the slightest sign of displeasure or anger, told Don to forget it. "Treat it like a fly on the end of your nose," he said. "Brush it off and go on about the important business before you." Don took the advice to heart and went back to planning the first full rally in Denver and the first summer conference.

January 1956 rolled around and the Fellowship was poised to take its message and its faith to the public in a person-to-person way. The first stop was Denver, where the FCA planned a 3-day citywide program.

The purpose of the first citywide rallies was clearly stated by the young body of Christians: One, to give young people the opportunity to meet and receive tips and advice from well-known athletes; and, two, to have the athletes share their Christian witness and to promote fellowship and a feeling of oneness in Christ with all the participants around the common bond of sports.

Gary Demarest had been selected as the master of ceremonies for these gatherings. And there were good reasons for the selection. He had, more than all the others, a strong, resonant voice that carried a message with a feeling of personal caring and conviction. Also, he was comfortable in front of large groups of people, whereas Don McClanen was not. And Demarest's selection was to put an imprint on one of the important aspects of the Fellowship. There were those men who brought their particular strengths to an area of endeavor in which others in the organization had a weakness. It was as though God had selected each of them with the care that a coach fills positions on a team—each had a necessary specialty to complement his teammates. And so this young and inexperienced team traveled to its first game in Denver.

Demarest was excited but also apprehensive as his plane from Princeton landed at the Denver airport. He knew that they were starting from scratch and guessing as to the most effective way to make their witness known. The plan seemed logical: gather a sufficient number of well-known college and professional athletes and coaches together and the audience would take care of itself.

Demarest arrived at the high school auditorium just 3 minutes before the program was to begin and he quickly realized that sometimes logic wasn't enough. There were about 25 athletes and coaches on the platform and hardly more people than that in the audience. It wasn't a good feeling. *Sports Illustrated* and 2 or 3 other national publications were on hand in the audience to cover this opening event. The turnout was meager. It was not an auspicious start and Gray was worried that the turnout might decrease for the following meetings.

But the program was carried out that afternoon in the auditorium and the logic of name athletes attracting young people was proven over the next several days as their numbers climbed into the hundreds. The participants breathed a collective sigh of relief.

In addition to the kickoff program in the high school auditorium, the athletes were scheduled to appear in high school assemblies during the next several days. The reaction of the students was enough to make the men glad to be a part of this unique ministry and assure them that they were traveling the right path. Learning from their first experience, they did advance work with the ministers and coaches in Houston, their next stop for 3 days in February 1956. The promotion paid off and the opening Sunday afternoon rally was packed full.

When the tired but buoyed athletes left Indianapolis in March 1956, the third and last stop on their initial city-wide program, an estimated 90,000 young people had met with members of the Fellowship of Christian Athletes, had asked questions ranging from tips on pitching curves and sliders to ways to perfect quicker football release for young quarterbacks. They also had heard—first-hand from their sports heroes—about the importance of a Christian life and attitude.

There were some moments that would give additional strength to this young team of Christians.

Palmer Hoyt, editor of the *Denver Post*, hosted a meeting of the visiting athletes, the *Post's* editorial staff, and Denver businessmen to learn first-hand what the Fellowship hoped to do.

At that meeting, after several athletes had spoken about the movement and why they had been attracted to it, Hoyt spoke up and said that he was, right then and there, contributing $1,000 to help insure more Fellowship visits to more young people. When Hoyt finished his comments, Carl A. Norgren, a Christian businessman, raised his hand and said that he would also donate $1,000. Two others also offered to help. McClanen's band of Christians left the Denver meeting with $2,400 to further the cause and to spread the word.

Another heartening note was added by the principal of the largest high school in Indianapolis, who wrote after the assembly in his school, "We have searched far and wide to secure speakers who can do the job the Christian athletes did. We seldom find them. . . ."

"Deacon" Dan Towler was touched in a personal way as deeply perhaps as anyone. An All-Pro running back for the Los Angeles Rams, he was one of the 19 men who had received McClanen's letter and he had been asked to be one of the professional athletes to appear in Denver. Towler spent 2 days in that city sharing with the hundreds of high school and college students what Jesus Christ meant in his life as a Christian athlete. It was a powerful experience for the football star and, as he was called on time and again to explain why he had dedicated his life to

Christ, he discovered that his own faith had grown much deeper.

There was another boost in the always-modest treasury. Glen Olds, the Methodist chaplain at Denver University who was an early joiner of the movement, knew an executive of the Danforth Foundation. That friendship and the powerful idea of the Fellowship resulted in a needed contribution from the Foundation. Additional financial gifts would soon come into the Fellowship's treasury as the result of men like Roe Johnston knocking on doors.

Johnston had called earlier on the Irwin-Miller-Sweeney Foundation. He had teamed with Biggie Munn, coach and athletic director at Michigan State, to call on potential donors. The Eli Lilly Foundation had received a call. And its belief in the movement soon became evident.

Munn had been loaned a small private plane by one of the Michigan State supporters and soon the plane had made stops at many of the state's airports. Biggie's reputation was the only calling card that was needed. Everyone, it seemed to Johnston, was glad to see the coach. Munn would chat a while about football at Michigan State, then introduce Johnston, and Johnston would outline the reason for their call and the financial need of the Fellowship.

The Kellogg Foundation was visited and became a donor to the Fellowship in 1957. Big and small businessmen were talked to and many gave.

Also in 1957, Roe Johnston's call on the Irwin-Miller-Sweeney Foundation was answered. As a result of Roe's contact, Richard Stoner had become an observer for J. Irwin Miller at a number of the Fellowship's meetings. He had been impressed with the men and the shared belief that the Fellowship was one in which committed lay persons could do some of God's work. He reported his reactions to Miller, who indicated how much he believed in the movement by donating $20,000, which strengthened the Fellowship in 1957. J. Irwin Miller, a trustee of Yale University, a Rhodes Scholar, and a concert violinist, was to go on the list of people who made a dream come true. The Fellowship's list of distinguished and concerned Christians was growing.

Encouraged by the reception in the citywide rallies, the men of the Fellowship now prepared for a more difficult test. Don McClanen had reserved enough campground space at the YMCA of the Rockies, Estes Park, Colorado, for 500 coaches and athletes. Four days in August 1956 had been set aside for the first national conference, which would include many well-known people in the sports world as leaders.

The 4 days were carefully blocked off to allow time for competitive sports, inspirational assemblies, workouts, re-laxation, and a chance for participants to reflect alone on what was being said and done by the men of the Fellow-ship to further serve Christianity and the church.

There was a statement of purpose for the conference: to confront athletes and coaches, and through them the youth of the nation, with the challenge and adventure of following Christ and serving Him through the fellowship of the church and in their vocations. There were speakers on behalf of the Fellowship: Branch Rickey; Dr. Evans; Doak Walker; Otto Graham; Bob Richards; Gary Demarest, always the master of ceremonies; and others. And there was some little-known groundwork laid at the highest level of leadership in the United States.

Dr. Evans was the summer pastor for President Dwight D. Eisenhower at National Presbyterian Church. Before the gathering at Estes Park, Dr. Evans told the President about the Fellowship. He saw the President's face light up: Like a Bunsen burner, Dr. Evans thought. Eisenhower was deeply involved in trying to formulate a program of moral and spiritual values for the nation's youth and he told Evans, "That's what we need. These athletes can remind youth that there is a goal in life and they can tell the young what that goal is."

Several Sundays before the conference was to start, Dr. Evans, from his place near the altar in National Presbyterian Church in Washington, called for prayers for this young group that was nearing the eve of its first national conference. Dr. Evans saw Secretary of State John Foster Dulles take a pencil and small notebook from his pocket.

"God, have him send a message of encouragement to these men," Evans prayed. And his prayer was answered. One of the first telegrams to arrive at Estes Park was from Eisenhower. It read:

Please give the delegates gathered at Estes Park my warm greetings. You will be invigorated for months ahead by the mountains around you and the devotion within you. I wish you a successful meeting.

Dwight Eisenhower

And on August 5 another wire was received, this one from Secretary of State Dulles. It read:

Dr. Louis Evans mentioned in his sermon ... your forth-coming gathering. I was delighted to hear of it. I feel confident that those of you who have won a reputation and influence in the field of athletics can equally exert Christian leadership and I am delighted that you are undertaking this. It will, I am sure, serve the interests of our nation which has from the beginning been strengthened by the Christian principle and its people.

Sincerely yours,
John Foster Dulles

But the messages from two of the nation's leaders weren't quite enough to dispel the Fellowship's concern

FCA officers in early 1960's (L to R): Tad Wieman, Denver U. athletic director; Dick Harp, Kansas U. basketball coach; pastor Dick Armstrong; and Paul Dietzel, football coach at Louisiana State.

Don Cockcroft, long-time placekicker and punter for the Cleveland Browns, at a conference in Estes Park.

about attendance.

"It has to be more than the last Denver meeting," thought Gary Demarest. "It has to." He rode from the Denver Airport to Estes Park with Branch Rickey, who wanted to know how many conferees would be in attendance. The actual pre-registration had been substantially less than 100, and Demarest and others felt that perhaps the Fellowship had made another mistake both because of the outstanding leadership that had been brought together to spearhead the conference, and also because *Sports Illustrated* would again be covering the event, as would *Life* magazine. He tried to evade an answer to Rickey's question, but Rickey persisted. When Demarest told him less than 100 had registered, Rickey couldn't hide his disappointment.

But both men soon were elated. They hadn't miscalculated. Many attendees had simply not registered in advance. A total of 256 coaches and athletes gathered for the opening session.

There were some loyal friends of the Fellowship in the audience along with young and old newcomers. Jim Stoner was there, sharing a room with Biggie Munn. James Jeffrey had driven from Texas with a carload of young athletes. Bill Krisher and Clendon Thomas were there as leaders of one of the groups of young athletes who competed and talked together throughout the conference. In keeping with the athletic theme of the conference, the term "huddle" was applied to such groups.

The man who was slated to give the keynote speech was Branch Rickey. It was a fitting tribute to the gravel-voiced baseball executive who had helped launch the movement, and his credentials were fitting tributes to the infant Fellowship.

Rickey, then 74, had a rich athletic past. He had played football and baseball in college, the same two sports as a professional, had been both a college coach and athletic director, and now was leading the Pirates. His major league career had been ended by tuberculosis after just 4 years and 119 games. Rickey had a deep Christian heritage, too. He was an outstanding Methodist layman who brought courage and character to whatever he did.

Nothing perhaps summed up Rickey's moral fiber as well as a story told by Carl Erskine:

Mr. Rickey always looked for what he called the 'red thread' of discipline, courage, confidence, and commitment to Christ in a man's life. He looked for it in every rookie he interviewed and if it were not there, he would look for qualities which might produce it.

There is one story that is little told about Jackie Robinson. Mr. Rickey had all the influence and prestige of his person and position to help get Robinson ready for the persecutions he would face. But instead Mr. Rickey took Jack into his office one day and read to him from Papini's *Life of Christ*. He explained the odds against Christ, the persecution he faced, how he was always right and seldom recognized as such and yet could turn the other cheek and have compassion and love for his worst enemies.

Armed with this, Jackie became Rookie of the Year and went on to the Hall of Fame. He became a 'Rickey Man,' a man armed with the 'red thread.'

And Jackie Robinson, a man of fiery temperament and competitiveness, learned from Rickey to turn the other cheek, to curb his resentment of criticism and not retaliate in kind. He honored Rickey with this statement:

"It isn't right to say I broke a color line. Mr. Rickey did. I played ball. Mr. Rickey made it possible for me to play. Of all the men I met in baseball, Mr. Rickey is the finest, in a class by himself."

That night in August 1956, Branch Rickey acknowledged

that he was in a class not by himself, but occupied by other deeply committed Christian men, the Fellowship of Christian Athletes.

His speech was stirring in its honesty, its conviction, and in its simple and eloquent belief. He talked of his parents, from whom he had been given the germ of his own Christian life. He noted:

They had something that wasn't in the books. They had no college degrees. They had never sat at the feet of a philosopher anywhere, but in the laboratory of experience. Down on bended knees on an uncarpeted kitchen floor, they had something that didn't need proof. Nobody could tell my father and my mother that there was no God. Neither could they tell them that Jesus was not the Son of God. They had quite enough. They had empirical knowledge, out of experience, and it worked.

Rickey talked of the Fellowship of Christian Athletes:

This Fellowship of Christian Athletes is not a physical conditioning process . . . it is a cooperative grouping of active athletes to embrace and have others embrace Jesus as the Christ, the measure of divinity through which we come to know and find God. It is an effort that challenges our best intelligence and all our emotions inside us. We must proceed to the task with conviction, with contriteness, and with courage even to the point of ardor.

He ended his talk with words aimed at every athlete, young and old, gathered at Estes Park:

I don't think I've ever been faced with a situation that seemed so pregnant with immediate possibilities of a great crowd of young men coming to feel the presence of God and the duty of service to the King of Kings.

That August night, with the Rocky Mountains in the background, Rickey played his most important game for the Fellowship of Christian Athletes.

But what Branch Rickey found in his heart to do was more difficult for some of the other prominent sports figures on hand to do that week. Don McClanen discovered that many of the athletes were more than willing to give their time and their presence, but that some of them felt awkward in witnessing their acceptance of Jesus Christ. Because it had not yet become easy for some of the men to openly share their feelings, Dr. Evans was called on to speak for the next 3 consecutive nights. He felt a personal thrill at the number of people in attendance. As McClanen had been led to him because of his Presbyterian ministry and his athletic background, so, too, were the young athletes led to hear his message.

Dr. Evans drew on his years of football as an All-State end at Occidental College and his years as a college and pro basketball player in California. He spoke of what an athlete the apostle Paul must have been, of how great a coach Jesus Christ was, of the challenge before the young people to help the church recapture the world from sin and return it to God again. He stressed the idea of the FCA in helping the church and left the participants with thoughts to ponder during "quiet time" the following days about their life and how the acceptance of Christ into that life could make their living a more worthwhile experience.

As Dr. Evans looked out over the 256 faces of athletes and coaches and remembered the telegrams from the President and Secretary of State, he thought to himself, "God has been good to us."

When the conference was over, there was a little time for reflection by those who had worked so hard. Donn Moomaw recalled how nervous and frightened the staff had been before the conference. But his thought was that the Fellowship was God's doing—not man's—and that he had blessed all of the workers and participants far beyond their wildest dreams.

Gary Demarest, unwinding from acting as dean for the entire conference, felt that the first national gathering had set the tone and the pace for such future meetings. He believed that there was virtue in holding to the same format for the future because so much good for Christ had been accomplished.

Roe Johnston also felt comfortable about the format. The conference had provided, in his opinion, a chance for high school and college athletes to meet with some of the people they looked up to and to find that these men were human beings, too, human beings of real conviction who weren't afraid to say so. And he believed that the personal associations that had taken place were going to be the real attraction for all of the participants in the future.

Rickey reflected that he had an almost boyish pride in belonging to the Fellowship.

But the impact of the conference wasn't confined to those men who had given birth to the Fellowship. It was best reflected in a note that came from a young participant at the end of the week. He wrote: "I came to the conference to see my gods; I heard my gods talking about their God and, when I left, their God was my God."

The impact reached beyond the conference grounds with the 500 spaces that Don McClanen had staked out.

A recent graduate of UCLA, an athlete on the football, baseball, and rugby field, Don Shinnick heard good things about the conference. He had already been introduced in an unorthodox way to the FCA while at UCLA. The Fellowship was making its first film, *More Than Champions*, and was shooting some scenes on the Bruins' campus. As Don Shinnick walked by the filming, someone grabbed him and several other students and asked them to serve as a kind of backdrop for the film. He hadn't paid enough attention to remember the name of the film.

But now he was paying attention. He had heard that 256 athletes and coaches had gathered in a place in Colorado and he got to wondering what the conference was all about and what all of the famous athletes were doing there. He looked more deeply into the conference and decided to add active service in the Fellowship to his future. Shinnick had already included in that future a linebacker spot with the Baltimore Colts.

The Fellowship had been blessed with help from those on the athletic field. Now it was the turn of a man who sat on the sidelines to assist the band of Christian brothers. Ernie Mehl, sports editor for the *Kansas City Star*, had been covering the A's in New York City and had attended Marble Collegiate Church to hear Norman Vincent Peale. In his sermon that Sunday, Dr. Peale made a reference to the courage of Carl Erskine, "a popular pitcher for the Brooklyn Dodgers who's recently joined an outfit called the Fellowship of Christian Athletes." Mehl approached Dr. Peale after the service to get more details about this organization that had attracted Erskine. Armed with information, Mehl traveled to Norman, Oklahoma, when the A's returned to their home park and he suggested to Don McClanen that the Fellowship should move its headquarters to a city that had a big-league team, and, as of the previous year, Kansas City had had a major league baseball team. He promised to help obtain the first office in Kansas City. It would be in the Professional Building, in the downtown section of the city.

McClanen agreed to accept Mehl's invitation and in September 1956, the Fellowship of Christian Athletes moved its headquarters to Kansas City. The move came one month after the national conference at Estes Park had boosted the organization into the national scene and into the lives of hundreds, then thousands, of athletes and coaches. It was now truly a fellowship. And a growing one.

THE CHURCH

The church, that great benefactor of Christian life, was itself to be the beneficiary of Don McClanen's dream. But there were times when that dream brought restlessness and uncertainty to the dreamer.

As Don McClanen wrestled with the problems of finance and organization, he also wrestled with a recurring question: Is this movement really something of God or isn't it? Through the early years, as he and the FCA concept were tested, Don began to find the answer. Yes, it was of God. As the idea and the work were brought to life, they forced him to grow as a true Christian. McClanen needed that bedrock of assurance that comes only from living a life for the Lord.

Before the church was to really benefit, to receive the fruits of FCA's labors, there was much questioning and debate among good men. Should the Fellowship, as had been suggested by the national television personality, be broader than a movement for just Christian athletes? It took the men of the church to firmly decide that issue. Dr. Evans spoke dramatically to that point. He told Don, as the issue reached near crisis, "If you take the 'C' out of this thing [the initials FCA], then you can take me out of it." It was Dr. Evans's bold witness to Jesus Christ and His church that decided the issue. The "C" remained. Roe Johnston also was firm in his commitment to the name and the purpose of serving the church.

No sooner had this issue been resolved than another crisis arose. What about the Roman Catholic Church? Don McClanen found himself pitted against thoughtful and conservative men who did not feel that the Fellowship and the Roman Catholic Church fit neatly together. McClanen argued that they did. With farsightedness and persuasion, he carried the argument. Out of the strength of debate among wise and dedicated men came the best kind of foundation for the Fellowship. It was a foundation that had been built on full and open exchange of viewpoints, on sometimes heated arguments, but always on the desire to do God's work.

When all the issues had been decided, they were decided with conviction and a knowledge that they were the right choices: The Fellowship would not compete with any denominations, but it would exist to serve Christ through the church. And the stated purpose of the organization would say, with trumpet-like authority, that it was: "A movement to present to athletes and coaches, all whom they influence, the challenge and adventure of receiving Jesus Christ as Savior and Lord, serving Him in their relationships and in the fellowship of the church."

As a testament to the vision of Don McClanen and his loyal comrades on the Roman Catholic issue, the Right Reverend Monsignor Donald Cleary, the chaplain at Cornell University, was asked and agreed to serve on one of

54

the first boards of directors of the Fellowship. One of his missions was to present the concept of the Fellowship to the Roman Catholic leadership and to the National Catholic Welfare Conferences. The reaction he received was more than encouraging. As he continued to labor for the Fellowship, he found that the years of experience, the growth of the ecumenical movement, and the increase of mutual trust resulted in the disappearance of the initial anxieties, with the result that the whole Fellowship idea and its implementation were received with favor by Catholic Church authorities whenever they were given a clear view of what the FCA was about.

Cleary worked hard on his mission. He knew that he had a worthwhile idea to convey. And he was successful. The Catholic priesthood and lay people began to participate more actively and more frequently. Some time after his involvement with the Fellowship at its grassroots level, this mid-West priest observed: "My involvement with the FCA has made me a better Catholic and a better priest."

The influence of the Fellowship in the life and the works of the church was almost preordained. The men who served it were dedicated men. McClanen was the driving force. Dr. Evans, pastor to thousands of people and also pastor to a President, brought his own sense of purpose in aiding the church. Roe Johnston, who had traded the uniforms of a football player and a shipboard Naval officer for the robes of the Presbyterian ministry, knew that the church should be served. Gary Demarest and Donn Moomaw, one a pastor headed back for graduate work at the Princeton Seminary and the other studying to enter the ministry, were committed to serving the church through the work of coaches and athletes. Two of the great business leaders who helped construct the financial underpinning of the infant Fellowship, Paul Benedum and J. Irwin Miller, were intimately involved in

A group of young athletes gather in a huddle at

a National Conference in Estes Park, Colorado.

57

the faith of men to the Lord. Irwin Miller became president of the National Council of Churches, a strong piece of evidence of his Christian faith.

Dan Towler, hard-charging running back for the Rams and one of the recipients of the original McClanen letter, attended his first summer conference in 1957. Along with him at that conference was his wife and their small daughter. Towler was then a member of the cloth and one of the few blacks involved with the McClanen dream. Towler was so moved by his experience and what he saw happen at that conference that he always thought of it as a miraculous week. He was so impressed with the program and the possibility of serving Jesus Christ through the Fellowship that he attended one or more conferences each summer during the next 17 years. As the current campus minister for Cal State in Los Angeles, he still attributes to the Fellowship the privilege that he and his family have had of meeting, learning, and growing in Christ with the thousands of coaches and other athletes who have attended FCA meetings through the years.

One of the most moving experiences for "Deacon" Dan Towler as a servant of the church came one early morning at a summer conference in the Rockies. The place was Estes Park. Towler was standing alone in a meadow behind the chapel, not far from the usual center of activities, watching the rising morning sun paint the mountains from their awesome heights down their sides.

A camper, a husky athlete, walked quietly up to him and, with the uneasy nervousness of someone in the presence of a person he admires, made just enough sound to interrupt Towler's thoughts. The "Deacon" recognized the young man as one of the boys who had shared in a small group discussion about the Lord the night before. As he spoke to Towler, the boy reached into one of his pants pockets, pulled out two rough-made brass knuckles, and extended them to the minister. "Mr. Towler," he said, "I

58

want to give you these. After what you told me about the man called Jesus last night, I don't need them anymore."

Dan Towler, like so many other men who wear the cleric's collar and labor with people for Christ, discovered that day that the Fellowship of Christian Athletes was more than a movement, that it was, in truth, people doing God's work.

And, of course, among the dedicated men, there was always (or so it seemed in the early days) the man rightly called Mr. Baseball, W. Branch Rickey, who lived quietly but effectively the life of the church. He gave his word, his work, and his private prayers to help the Fellowship become a path of travel to the church. He was a man of God and a man of Christian heritage. His father in 1880 had begun building a little church in the hills of Southern Ohio. He built it with the help of the people in the small settlement, away from the railroad and the highways. Branch Rickey remembered it as a church without name, a sort of community church. But from it and from his parents' side he learned what a life for Christ could bring in the way of spiritual reward and a feeling of worth.

Rickey, a man who was to play and to coach and to revolutionize the sport of baseball, grew up promising his mother and his father that he would never go to a ball park on a Sunday. And he never did. Jimmy Austin became Rickey's "Sunday manager" when Rickey was secretary, then manager, of the St. Louis Browns in the old American League. Rickey never came to the park on a Sunday, but rather put Austin in charge. Rickey never prayed in public; he stayed with his family at home. But, before the 256 assembled athletes, coaches, and Christians, on the night when the Fellowship launched its first summer conference, at the foot of the Rockies, Rickey did pray aloud. And when he was finished with his speech, when the crowd of participants was still quiet in the awe of his words and his devotion to a Christian life, he added softly before he took his seat, "Amen."

Rickey was so committed to helping the church through the Fellowship that he wrote down his innermost feelings about the worth of the idea following his initial 5-hour meeting with Don McClanen. He handed the young Oklahoma coach what he had written and told Don to use those thoughts as a calling card whenever he felt the need. McClanen remembers Rickey always stressing that the Fellowship work within the church. And it did from the outset.

There were and there are legions who stand and work as exciting examples of the bond between the Fellowship and the church.

Dick Armstrong was the public-relations official for the Baltimore Orioles when Don McClanen looked to him for aid in putting a funding base together for the just-born idea. Armstrong, who later went to Princeton Seminary, played a major role in the drafting and adoption of the Fellowship's constitution. He remembers helping to shape and direct Don's dream. He was part of the group who spent long hours as members of the first board of directors, meeting at Estes Park, to hammer out the philosophical foundation for a program that he and many of his co-workers believed was inspired by God and only entrusted to men as stewards. It was during those long and tiring but fulfilling hours that the first board determined that the Fellowship of Christian Athletes should be directly related to and supportive of the church.

Julian Dyke, the driver of one of the cars carrying a cargo of young athletes to the first national conference and later vice-president of the Fellowship for 9 years, also was a living bridge between the Fellowship and the church. Dyke had been a person whose life was to find a dominant and consistent influence in the church. The Fellowship became one of the most profound influences in his life, helping him keep active his interest and his learning as a Christian through the church. It was Dyke's personal message when he worked as an officer in the Fellowship in the formative years that served as a clear call to all who recognized the church. "We don't care," he was fond of saying, "whether an athlete or coach is Catholic, Baptist, Presbyterian, Lutheran, Pentecostal, or whatever. What we hope is that through his participation with the Fellowship he will become a more enthusiastic and committed churchman in his own congregation."

The striving of McClanen and his band to resolve the question of an ecumenical approach for the Fellowship has continued to reap benefits for the church. Dr. Ernest Gordon, chaplain at Princeton University, was to be a spokesman for the wisdom of the decision. "What I have found," he testified, "is that it's a fellowship which is honestly ecumenical and honestly Christian."

And through the years, as the Fellowship of Christian Athletes sowed the message, churches reaped. And many who have stood Sunday after Sunday in the pulpits of the nation and led congregations in prayer were aware of the Fellowship's good works.

John Robertson, pastor of the First Presbyterian Church in Carthage, Missouri, attended a gathering of the athletes when they came to his community. When they left that small dot on the map near the Oklahoma-Kansas-Missouri border, they had left an indelible impression on John Robertson. He committed that impression to paper:

Here in America we are having packed stadiums and crowded golf courses but only half-filled churches. The hero of the day is no longer the pastor, preacher, or pulpiteer. It is the quarterback, the pitcher, the miler. The champion is not the testifier or teller of the Good News but the well-padded and well-paid maker of sports news. However, the Fellowship of Christian Athletes is changing all this. . . .

Fellowship in sport.

Don Shinnick, linebacker for the Baltimore Colts.

The FCA is one of God's means through which a congregation can be renewed and revitalized as men and boys, active athletes and sports spectators share with others the "challenge and adventure of following Christ through the fellowship of the church." This is FCA's intent and purpose and for this, we praise God.

Others, too, have shared the worth and the meaning of this special ministry of athletes and coaches.

The Reverend Ron Davis is the pastor of Hope Presbyterian Church in Minneapolis, Minnesota, and was twice the high school cross-country champion of Iowa. The difference between the young boy running in measured stride across Iowa fields and the man who leads one of God's flocks was a decision and a course of study at Dubuque Theological Seminary in Dubuque, Iowa. He has a keen insight into what good works can be done in the name of Jesus Christ by athletes who are Christians. Ron has written: "The athlete has something going for him. . . . Because I have an athletic background, the youth of my church seem to relate to me. Too many of our seminary products offer youth no real masculine attraction."

There were also those who went from athletic competition to the sanctuary of the church because of the impact of the Fellowship on their lives. The stories are numerous, each with a personal beauty of fulfillment.

Stimp Hawkins, a Virginia high school football coach, attended a national summer conference in 1964. Shortly after returning to Virginia, and reflecting on the message of other coaches and athletes (some of whose names he had known and some of whom he met for the first time and came to respect), he entered Union Theological Seminary in Richmond, Virginia.

Tony Howard was twice a state wrestling champion in Oklahoma, where the Fellowship was born. His involvement with the movement, his association with people he respected for their physical abilities and later for their spiritual strengths, changed his life. He decided on a life for the Lord in 1963.

Merline Batt, a standout major league prospect, attended two of the Fellowship's conferences at Henderson Harbor, New York. When he returned from the second one, he changed his major at Johns Hopkins University in order to prepare for the study of theology.

David Bryan, an honorable-mention All-American basketball player at the University of Chattanooga, entered Columbia Seminary at Decatur, Georgia, after the message of the Fellowship entered his life.

Deep skepticism was turned to deep belief for Max Stratton, who attended one of the early conferences in Estes Park. The year was 1959. Stratton was coach of a Kansas high school football team that had a less than impressive record. When a fellow coach invited him to go with him to Estes Park, Stratton told him in language that coaches understand: "Look, I'm having enough trouble winning with red-blooded athletes; I don't need any of that sissy stuff." As was the case in so many other homes and as had been the case with the man who started it all, Don McClanen, there was a wife who loved and cared. Max Stratton's wife urged him to go to the conference, encouraged him to go, then finally paid his way. Stratton traveled west to Colorado. With him was his young quarterback, a student named Don Kuhlman. Otto Graham was on the program at Estes Park and Stratton felt that both he and his young signal-caller could possibly profit from meeting with Graham and getting some first-hand tips.

The original purpose was thwarted; they did not get to meet Graham. But they both found a higher purpose during the 5 days at the conference. Before they began the long trip home, Max and Don knelt in the rustic chapel at the conference site and asked God to lead their lives.

One year later, Max Stratton, 35, former high school football coach, husband of a woman who cared deeply for him, entered St. Paul's School of Theology in Kansas City, Missouri. He became a pastor of a United Methodist Church and in 1967 attended a homecoming of special significance: He joined the staff of the Fellowship of Christian Athletes as its Central Plains regional director.

The young quarterback who went to Estes Park with Max Stratton and found that the journey led to greater and higher places than just a spot where he might meet a professional quarterback also entered the ministry. Don Kuhlman is now the pastor at Bethany Lutheran Church in Minden, Nebraska.

Len LeSourd had helped McClanen by giving him copies of *Guideposts* articles on the great athletes of the day. He had helped push to completion the first brochures of the movement to give it exposure. Len also had given the tremendous influence of *Guideposts* freely to call attention to the first conference at Estes Park. He found a reward in 1961 at Estes Park. That year he persuaded his stepson, Peter Marshall, to attend a summer conference shortly after Peter's graduation from Yale. The young man had a deep Christian heritage, against which he was in full rebellion at the time, LeSourd knew. Young Peter was the son of the famous former chaplain of the United States Senate and one of the nation's noted authors, Catherine Marshall, who wrote *A Man Called Peter*.

The Yale graduate told his mother and stepfather that he would go, but that he would head for the nearest bar if the gathering got religious. He never needed the bar. Peter was assigned, with other young men, to a huddle group led by Donn Moomaw. One night in one of the lounges, with a few others gathered nearby, Donn Moomaw and Gary Demarest confronted the man from Yale with the fact that he had to make a decision one way or another about Jesus Christ. Peter Marshall didn't believe in the inheritance of Christianity; he believed and came to know that in his life there had to be a personal encounter between himself and Christ for it to mean anything. Six weeks after the conference ended, Peter Marshall, graduate of Yale, former rebel against his Christian background, enrolled in Princeton Seminary.

LeSourd was to receive again from the Fellowship that he helped to launch. Seven years after Peter's moving experience, Len LeSourd, his 15-year-old son Chet, and his other son Jeff attended a national conference at Black Mountain, North Carolina. Late one night Chet lay in his bed, thinking about a discussion about Jesus that he and several other young men had just finished. He turned over in bed and suddenly sat up. Standing by the door to his small room was the person of Jesus. The 15-year-old boy carried on a brief conversation, which the person of Jesus ended by telling him, "You are to be one of my missionaries." Then He was gone.

The next morning Chet sought out his father and excitedly, almost breathlessly, told him what had happened. The age of 15 is not too young for the understanding of a father's words about a Christian life. Len LeSourd and his son talked and they both agreed that missionary work for Jesus Christ could be done in any profession in the world. It depended on the professional. Chet developed two great skills as he matured through high school and college: the game of tennis and the ability to relate to young people. In 1979 Chet began his mission at McCallie School in Chattanooga, Tennessee, a preparatory school for boys, where he teaches English and coaches tennis.

The Fellowship has been true to its purpose. It has funneled coaches and athletes and those whom they influence into the church and into a Christian way of life. More than 125 men who have played or coached on athletic fields throughout the country have entered seminaries across this land because they have been directly touched by one of the Fellowship's endeavors.

Bob Pettit was one of the early giants in the movement and one of the living legends of the basketball court. He was the first man in professional basketball history to score 20,000 points as a forward for the St. Louis Hawks. Pettit speaks in simple yet eloquent and understanding language of the FCA and its commitment to the Church:

At every important point in my life I've turned to the church and to Christ and found the kind of help I couldn't find anyplace else. That's why I'm glad that a central purpose of the FCA is to support and strengthen the church.

What Don McClanen sensed only vaguely in 1947 and what he nurtured for 7 years and what a number of good men believed in and worked for is truly a fellowship.

Of Christians.

Who happen to be athletes and who happen to be coaches but men who are first and foremost Christians.

OF
ATHLETES
AND
COACHES

Stadiums. From the imposing grandeur of the Rose Bowl in Pasadena, California, to the modest bleachers in Gurness, Illinois, these structures contain the seedbed of man's ageless desire to compete and to excel in disciplines of the body.

The nation knew in 1954 that America had been infected by the worship of these athletes. Their pictures appeared on billboards, in magazines, in newspapers. They endorsed and helped to sell everything from breakfast food to toothpaste to automobiles. But only Don McClanen knew in 1954, with the conviction of a man doing God's work, that the athletes and the men who coached them could be a help in promoting a Christian way of life. And at the outset, he knew only that 14 men had taken pen in hand to promise him their time, physical presence, and perhaps their witness.

Behind those 14 commitments and the thousands that were to come is a special kind of courage. Roe Johnston summed it up, from his perspective as an athlete and a minister: "In the early days the concept was for those who were church people to say to the unchurched that it takes a real man to be a disciple of Christ; it isn't sissy."

Carl Erskine, among the original group of athletes, knew just how difficult Don's mission would be. The idea, at the time McClanen explained it to him in a hotel lobby, was really out of step with the times. The clubhouses, Erskine knew, were not places that were conducive to spiritual direction. That was all very private. If an athlete wanted to develop his faith or brought it with him from his background into pro sports, he was identified with it, but his religion was usually a subtle, behind-the-scenes thing. With the help of the Fellowship of Christian Athletes and the courage of their convictions, athletes throughout the country today openly, but without ostentation, serve the Lord. Some do it more easily than others for a variety of reasons.

It came easier for Bill Krisher, because of his Christian heritage and his acceptance of the Lord at 9 years of age. When he heard first-hand in the fall of 1954 about the Fellowship in the freshman athletic dorm at the University of Oklahoma, he sensed there was a role for him. After Bill and his college roommate and football teammate, Clendon Thomas, heard Otto Graham and Doak Walker tell of the excitement and the potential of the organization, both became active members. Krisher was invited during his sophomore year in late 1955 to be one of the athletes appearing and speaking in Indianapolis for a weekend to generate understanding and support for the as-yet-unnamed movement.

He was one of the leaders of the high school students at the first national conference, and he gave the time that he had away from the football field and the classroom to speak on behalf of the Fellowship throughout the state of Oklahoma. And Oklahomans listened. Krisher by then had been named to the first of 2 years on the All-American football team and the University of Oklahoma was the home of the national champions of college football, first in 1955 and again in 1956.

Krisher continued blocking for the Fellowship after he was graduated from Oklahoma and moved into the professional ranks as offensive guard with the Pittsburgh Steelers. He left an enviable college athletic record: twice All-American and 3 times All-Conference in the Big Eight. And he was making new records, both on the pro field and in the work of the Fellowship. For the 2 years with the Steelers, he worked in the off-season to assist in the maturing of the McClanen dream and he had the opportunity to know and to associate with another man who believed in the merits of the dream, Paul Benedum, who was to become a deep and close friend.

In 1960, Bill Krisher left the City of Steel for Big D, Dallas, Texas. He joined the Dallas Texans, whose football fame in that city has been now eclipsed by Tom Landry and Company. He played for the Texans in 1960 and 1961 and then resigned to answer what he knew was the call of the Lord. He signed on full-time with the organization that now had the name Fellowship of Christian Athletes. The offices then were in Kansas City and Krisher continued to combine the world of athletics with the spiritual world. In addition to working with the 3-man FCA national staff, he also found time to assist in bringing the Dallas Texans to Kansas City. The new location meant a new name: the Kansas City Chiefs. Krisher had been recognized while still on the team by being selected All-Pro.

Bill stayed with FCA until 1965, when he took 3 years off and went to Vermont. He returned in 1968, again in a full-time capacity. He is now regional director for the Fellow-

Pole Vaulter Brian Sternberg as a U. of Washington sophomore.

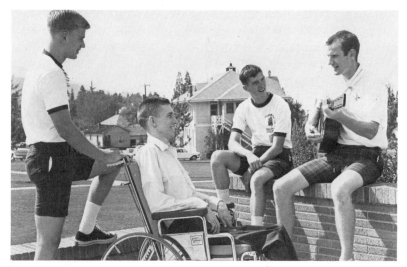

Sternberg, left paralyzed by a trampoline accident, continued his interest in FCA. He is shown here in 1966 with Wes Wilmer (standing), track star Gerry Lindgren and FCA staff member Ray Hildebrand.

Olympic Decathlon champion Rafer Johnson visits with young FCA members.

ship of Christian Athletes in Texas, Arizona, New Mexico, Arkansas, and Oklahoma, the state where his football greatness and his belief in the Fellowship were born.

For others, work for the Fellowship and the open expression of their witness was not an easy thing at first. Raymond Berry was such a man. His first exposure to the Fellowship was in the early spring of 1960. He was by then 5 years into a career with the Baltimore Colts that would lead him to selection as an All-Pro 3 times, as a player in 6 Pro Bowls, and as a member of the Hall of Fame in 1973.

Professional football fans had come to accept as commonplace the image of No. 82, body extended sometimes parallel, sometimes perpendicular to the ground, but always in mid-air with fingers always cementing themselves to passes from Unitas.

Raymond Berry in the spring of 1960 was a drawing card for tens of thousands. He was asked, because of that wide appeal, to appear as part of a Fellowship program in Texas over a weekend.

Although a member of a church, he had no real knowledge then of a personal relationship with God through Jesus Christ. He went to Texas because he had been asked to go. His mind was on other things—the woman he'd just met, who was later to become his wife.

But in July of that year, Berry met Christ for the first time. The Fellowship of Christian Athletes took on meaning for Ray as a vehicle through which he met other Christians and he had an opportunity to share his faith.

For the next 7 years, this former Southern Methodist University star brought thousands to their feet with his special kind of magic as a Baltimore receiver. Then he stepped down as a player and began a coaching career in professional football that continues today. Throughout the years, when the family and the career have allowed, he has shared his experiences with young and old in the gatherings of the Fellowship.

Another athlete who came slowly, but deliberately, into the folds of the Fellowship was Alan Ameche. Heisman Trophy Winner in 1954 as a fullback for Wisconsin, he was called "The Horse," and he was the Baltimore Colts' first-round draft choice in 1954. And if he moved slowly toward the rewards of the Fellowship, he moved with an awesome power on the field. He made the Colts squad in his rookie year and on the team's first play from scrimmage in their season opener against the Bears, Ameche took the ball, thundered through a gaping hole in the line, and churned his powerful legs to a touchdown 79 yards distant. It was an auspicious debut to a career that was to see him named All-Pro from 1955 through 1959.

When he wasn't listening to signals being called and the adulation of the crowds on the field, Ameche found himself listening to 2 teammates, Raymond Berry and Don Shinnick, talk about an organization called the Fellowship of Christian Athletes.

Ameche was a Roman Catholic who had attended Mass all his life and the idea of the Fellowship really didn't catch on with him. He didn't feel committed enough to give up a lot of his time to meet and to talk with young people. He acknowledged to himself that those in the Fellowship had put their Christianity on the line, but he simply wasn't ready.

It took a second effort in Alan Ameche's life to have him walk the final distance into the Fellowship. A retired naval officer who had been stationed outside Philadelphia, where Ameche had entered business after retiring from the Colts, asked him to help generate some local interest in the Fellowship. Ameche began giving his time, then went to hear Bob Vogel, a former Baltimore Colts lineman, share his experiences with the FCA.

It was after this encounter that Ameche accepted the challenge of heading the FCA effort in the Philadelphia area. That effort continues to reap great rewards. As a

Bill Krisher of the Pittsburgh Steelers works through some exercises with a college wrestler.

Raymond Berry, spokesman for the FCA.

Raymond Berry, the All-Pro end for the Baltimore Colts.

result of his FCA experience, Alan Ameche helped develop a Bible study group that meets once a month in his home. Anywhere from 6 to 20 men gather to share their Christian feelings and discuss Scripture.

Ameche acknowledges that he went through a very difficult transition from being the tough-talking, tough-acting fullback in college and pro ball to a gentler kind of man and a more thoughtful Christian. The Bible study group that gathers in his home has opened up new vistas for him. He had always considered himself a Christian, had always attended Mass. But there is a new dimension in Alan Ameche's life and there has been since the first meeting of these men 7 years ago. He is more able to talk about his faith, to share those things that at one time he considered to be very private. He has heightened his feelings about Christ, saying that he now thinks of Christ more as a brother than a father image. It is another example of the Fellowship of Christian Athletes working and sharing—sharing with each other and sharing in God's victory.

Bob Richards, the man who literally soared to gold medals in the Olympics as the United States' competitor in the pole vault, became another fine example of sharing his physical prowess and his spiritual strength. High school students, who began to meet in organized FCA " huddle" groups during 1966, listened with keen intent to Richards talk to them in language they could understand: "Christianity is not creeds, doctrines, and high-flown academic words. Christianity is faith in the hearts of people. . . . I love the sport world because you have to act on your faith. It is so easy in other institutions to let someone else do the job, but in sports nobody else can do it for you. . . ."

In athletics, whether on the hard sod of a rural football field or the paint-book green of the artificial surfaces in college and professional stadiums, no one can hold a position quite like a coach. His influence is enormous. His guidance and his leadership on the field and off the field is perhaps unique to the athletes who labor for him. It was with this knowledge in mind that coaches became one of the two foundations of the Fellowship's ministry. Like the athletes, some coaches responded quickly, others more slowly. But when each in his own way had made a commitment to the FCA, the organization and thousands of lives were the richer for it.

Dick Harp, a Kansas City, Kansas, product, showed up at the University of Kansas the fall of 1936 and turned out for the freshman basketball team. "Who's that guy?" the legendary "Phog" Allen asked somebody.

"That guy" ended up to be a 3-year starter for the Jayhawks and one of the standout players in the school's illustrious basketball history. Dick's tenacious defense and timely shooting helped spark the Jayhawks to 2 conference championships. His senior year he co-captained a strong Kansas team which finished runner-up to Indiana in the NCAA tournament.

Following an army stint in World War II, Dick launched his basketball coaching career at William Jewell College in Liberty, Missouri, and then returned to the University of Kansas in 1948 where he served as assistant to Coach Allen for 8 years.

One morning the fall of 1956, Dick was sorting out Coach Allen's mail when he noticed the letters "F.C.A." in the upper left-hand corner of the envelope. "Hey, someone's using your name," he kidded Coach Allen whose actual appellation was Forest C. Allen.

The letter was from Don McClanen, inviting Phog to speak to a group of high school coaches at an upcoming FCA program in Nashville, Tennessee. Unbeknown to Dick, Coach Allen had both attended and spoken at the inaugural FCA Conference at Estes Park that previous June. But now he was immersed in pre-season practice and urged Dick to take his place.

The timing couldn't have been better. Harp had been seeking a more meaningful and active faith life and this seemed a perfect avenue. He traveled to Nashville and addressed the coaches, little suspecting that someday he would serve as the glue holding the diverse FCA movement together.

Coach Allen resigned not long afterwards and Dick replaced him. He also attended the second FCA National Conference at Estes Park that next summer, became a member of FCA's National Advisory Board in 1958 and a member of the Board of Directors in 1959 to which he was named first vice-president in 1963.

Meantime Coach Harp's 1957-1958 squad, led by a fellow named Wilt Chamberlain, whipped 3 opponents in the NCAA playoffs before losing the national championship to North Carolina in 3 overtimes. He enjoyed 4 winning seasons in his 8 years at the helm, copping the conference title twice and compiling a 120-82 record. Many coaches would gladly take those figures but Dick was inevitably compared to Allen, who had enjoyed enormous success in 39 seasons, and alumni pressure began to mount.

Dick resigned the spring of 1964 to become managing director for FCA at its Kansas City headquarters. Besides his consuming coaching duties at KU, he'd sponsored the FCA Fellowship group on campus, helped send local athletes to Conference, and spoken at numerous FCA occasions throughout the state.

Serving as managing director was a natural extension of his increasing love for FCA and he was the backbone of the Fellowship in the mid-1960s as it emerged into both a movement and an organization of national significance. His strength, wisdom and leadership capacity were most firmly felt when he acted as interim executive director during a difficult transition period between executive directors in the early 1970s.

During Dick's tenure with FCA, 12 to 16 hour days and a totally committed lifestyle have been the rule of thumb rather than the exception. His influence opened doors to scores of coaches who became involved in FCA, and his behind-the-scenes role in recent years as FCA executive vice president has been largely responsible for the culmination of the Fellowship's new headquarters building.

Dick Harp, probably more than any other individual in FCA, has modeled himself on Jesus' injunction to be "a good and faithful servant."

Dan Stavely had just arrived at the University of Colorado as freshman football coach from a similar job at Washington State University. He read a story in the *Denver Post* about an organization that was new to him, the Fellowship of Christian Athletes. The story explained that the organization was conducting a summer conference at Estes Park, Colorado, not far from his new coaching home in Boulder, Colorado, and listed the names of some of the participants: Branch Rickey, Bud Wilkinson, and Carl Erskine. Dan Stavely, a young coach, thought to himself: "This is something I ought to be taking in." So he went to the conference alone that first summer of 1957.

That first experience, born of a curiosity to see what it was all about and to meet some of the great names in the sports world, became a lasting part of Dan Stavely's life. He returned to the conference the next summer, this time with some of his football players. In the fall of 1958 he started a FCA group on the Colorado campus; that chapter today is one of the largest in the country.

Dan Stavely retired in May 1979, after 22 years as the freshman football coach, academic adviser, and assistant athletic director of the university. But he hasn't retired from the university's Fellowship ministry and he doesn't intend to. He feels that the FCA has blessed him tremen-

Former FCA President James Jeffrey, flanked by former Oregon Governor Mark Hatfield. "Jeff" was an All-Southwest conference halfback at Baylor and active in student affairs. His tenure was one of growth and inspiration for FCA.

Former Kansas University basketball coach Dick Harp, currently
the executive vice president of
the FCA.

Bob Stoddard, FCA President
1962-1963

Former Brooklyn Dodger ace Carl Erskine, one of the FCA's early supporters, is currently a Board of Trustees member. Here he offers tips.
Carl's son, Jimmy, afflicted with mongolism, stands by his father.

dously: he's gotten to know men like Tom Landry, Paul
Dietzel, and many others in a very personal way.

His reflections are moving in their simplicity:

Where else would a fellow like me, an assistant, get on
first-name speaking terms with men like Tom Landry, for
instance? There's just no way except through this brother-
hood of Christ. When we sit down around a table, the difference in coaching status that exists is gone, and we're
just two men seeking to have a little better relationship
with the Lord.

Paul Dietzel, who was to become one of the shirt-sleeve
workers of the Fellowship, was introduced to the
organization in 1958, when he was head football coach at
Louisiana State University. It was a year that LSU was
declared National Champion in football. And on January
1, 1959, Paul Dietzel took his squad into the Sugar Bowl at
New Orleans and emerged a 7–0 winner over a stubborn
Clemson team. Later in 1959, Dietzel's famed halfback,
Billy Cannon, was to receive the Heisman Trophy. Dietzel
left LSU, coached at West Point, then at South Carolina,
and finally returned to LSU as athletic director. Throughout the years, he gave his time and his effort to the
Fellowship. When he was asked a few years ago by a
newspaper reporter what he, as a coach, thought was the
greatest thing that had happened in football during the
past decade, he did not hesitate in answering: "The
greatest thing that has happened in athletics in the last
two decades is the Fellowship of Christian Athletes."

Sometimes it was the men who hadn't made a team or
coached who became the apostles of the Fellowship on a
campus. One such man was Frank Hart Smith, whose influence on behalf of the FCA continues today.

Smith, who picked up the nickname "Pogo" by frequently quoting to his high school and college charges from the comic strip character of that name, was working at a church in Waco, Texas—the Seventh and James Baptist Church, across the street from the Baylor University campus. A friend of Smith's, James Jeffrey, told Smith about the Fellowship and the two men agreed that the organization might be worthwhile for some of the Baylor University and local high school students in Smith's care. He talked with a member of the church; the churchman contributed enough money for "Pogo" and 3 young men to go to Estes Park in 1959. Smith returned excited and he shared his excitement with John Bridgers, then football coach at Baylor. Bridgers went to a conference and he, too, returned impressed with the mission of the Fellowship.

"Pogo" Smith started an FCA group on the Baylor campus. That group, in turn, was invited by a group of young men at the University of Texas to visit the Austin campus and one more Fellowship on another campus was formed.

Smith left Waco in 1962 for a position with the Sunday School Board, the national publishing house of the Southern Baptist Convention. He hadn't been in Nashville long before he had started a Fellowship group on the Vanderbilt University campus. He has remained adviser to that chapter for 16 years. Those 16 years have been to Frank Hart Smith the most meaningful in his life, for he has been "seeing young men come to the Lord and seeing them really care about each other and just seeing God work on that campus and seeing what happens in their lives after they leave college."

Some helpers were coaches and others were athletes. And some were like Frank Hart Smith: "I was the oldest of four boys. The other three were very good natural-born athletes. Me, I was just a little too small." Too small for football perhaps, but large in the eyes of the Lord.

85

(L to R): Bart Starr, Lamar Hunt, and Tom Landry at an FCA weekend in Dallas, Tex., 1969.

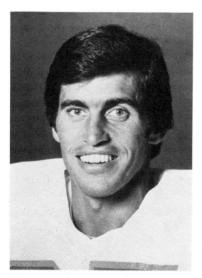

Miami Dolphin linebacker Tim Foley.

All-pro linebacker Randy Gradishar.

Gradishar in pursuit with Denver Broncos.

Tom Landry, at work with Dallas Cowboys.

Julian Dyke was a high school football coach in Baltimore, Maryland. In 1960 Billy Hunter, then on the coaching staff of the Baltimore Orioles, invited Dyke to pick some of his top high school players and go to a Fellowship conference in Lake Geneva, Wisconsin. Dyke accepted. He and another Baltimore high school coach drove two carloads of young men from Maryland to Wisconsin.

Dyke accepted Hunter's invitation for purely selfish reasons. He was a high school coach and he found that Bill Murray, then at Duke, Paul Dietzel, Dave "Boo" Ferriss of the Boston Red Sox, and Bob Feller, former great with the Cleveland Indians, would be there. Dyke was going in order to soak up as much coaching information as he could, a reason that brought many coaches to their first conference.

Julian Dyke soaked up more than he bargained for at his first conference. He remembers a car, old and crumpled around the fenders, pulling up in front of his own vehicle when he arrived. A group of Southern kids from Georgia were inside. The kid driving the car, he remembers, was kind of small—a small kid by the name of Fran Tarkenton. Dyke remembers seeing a young high school basketball player from Crystal City, Missouri, who'd come to get some counsel from Bob Pettit. A skinny kid, with a broken leg. His name was Bill Bradley. Bill went on to star at Princeton, be named a Rhodes scholar, and return to the States to become an All-Star with the New York Knicks. Today he is Senator Bill Bradley, but he still retains those values and beliefs that he shared as a high school participant in the conference "huddles."

Julian Dyke returned from that first conference with an idea, the same idea that so many other coaches of young men brought home: How to build a better life for himself and for those he influenced as a coach. Going to the conference was as important an experience as he was to have.

He had been at the conference just a few days when he became aware that many of the people there had something that he did not possess. He had gone to the conference as a coach, but not as a Christian. He wasn't sure what the others had, something indefinable, but he knew that he wanted it—the peace of mind, the sureness about life, the sense of purpose, the love. He began searching.

When he returned to his Baltimore home, Julian shared his feelings with his wife. His experience with the Fellowship became important to both of them and they became more active in their church. Julian gave leadership to the college Fellowship group in the Baltimore area and he assisted in founding an adult chapter. And about a year after his drive to Wisconsin, he helped start a weekly prayer breakfast each Tuesday with men like himself, who were interested in athletic and spiritual growth.

And one year almost to the day after he and his fellow Baltimore coach made the 2-car trip to Lake Geneva, Wisconsin, with a small collection of hand-picked young athletes, a chartered bus, completely filled with coaches and athletes, pulled out of the bus station in Baltimore. Its destination: a national conference of the Fellowship of Christian Athletes in Lake Geneva.

Tom Landry, in his second year as head coach of the Dallas Cowboys, was introduced to the Fellowship of Christian Athletes in 1962. He had moved from his position as defensive coach of the New York Giants to the spanking-new Cowboys in 1960. Since that move, his record as a coach and the record of his players as a team have become part of the lore of professional football.

It was while he was with the Giants that Tom Landry had accepted Jesus Christ as his Savior. He had, with some misgivings and almost no enthusiasm, begun to attend a Bible study group each Wednesday. The Giants had just come from the championship game with the Baltimore Colts—to Coach Landry and to thousands of others, one of the greatest games ever played. But he sensed that his life was not complete. From that Bible study class came his acceptance of Jesus Christ.

Landry accepted an invitation in 1962 to attend an FCA conference at Estes Park. He was amazed to find more than 700 coaches and athletes in attendance, participating in sports and sharing athletic and spiritual experiences. He knew after that week that the Fellowship would be an effective vehicle for sharing his faith with young athletes. He has remained true to that conviction, lending a highly respected name in professional football and a deep and abiding faith to the Fellowship.

The Fellowship's foundation, now strong, was given an even more substantial underpinning in 1969 when an annual conference was initiated for coaches and their wives.

Coaches of all sports at all levels and, importantly, their wives and children, gathered for the first annual National Coaches Conference at Estes Park. One of those coaches, who was to conduct a clinic for his peers, was Dean Smith, who had become head basketball coach at the University of North Carolina in 1962. Smith had just coached his Carolina team to the second consecutive Eastern Regional NCAA Championship and was to return from Estes Park and take them to a third Eastern regional championship, a feat never previously or subsequently accomplished by a coach.

With the launching of the coaches' conference, the Fellowship of Christian Athletes offered an unique combination of coaching advice and spiritual leadership.

The fifth birthday of the conference, in the summer of 1973, was a prime example. It was a Who's Who of the coaching world. Grant Teaff, head football coach at Baylor and the 1972 Southwest Conference Coach of the Year, led a clinic for fellow coaches on effective communications. Included in his checklist were an open-door policy, interviews with each player, entertaining black and white players and their wives at home, team devotionals before each game, and daily staff devotionals.

Nebraska football coach Tom Obsorne told the 400 coaches that they needed to help their athletes see themselves from the coach's perspective, that coaches had an obligation to sit down with players and talk honestly about their performances and the areas in which the players needed to improve.

Dick Schultz, basketball coach at Iowa, said it was his practice to tell all of his players that he would be involved with their personal as well as their athletic lives.

Sam Bell, track coach at Indiana, shared his philosophy: "I tell my athletes that I recruit them for life—not just for four years. I never take a young man on a scholarship unless I've visited with him in his home."

And there were others there to give advice and offer guidance: Ken Hayes, basketball, Tulsa; Bill Battle, football, Tennessee; Carl Erskine, baseball, Anderson (Indiana); and assistant coaches from both Baylor and Tennessee.

Before the 400 men and their families left that fifth conference, Bill Battle, one of the country's youngest and most successful football coaches, stood before the final assembly and told of how much the conference had meant to him and how he hoped to help in starting a similar conference on the East Coast.

And in 1977 the Fellowship's conferences for coaches did, in fact, stretch the breadth of the land—from Black Mountain, North Carolina, in the East, through Granby, Colorado, to San Diego, California, in the West. But the meaning and the mission of the Fellowship continued in only one direction: toward richer and fuller Christian lives.

Coaches heard the call of the Fellowship in a variety of ways, now that the organization had taken root and was growing.

Ed McNeil, a high school coach in Fort Dodge, Iowa, came to know the Fellowship through a strange set of circumstances. One of his friends in Fort Dodge, an insurance salesman, picked up a copy of the Fellowship's magazine, The *Christian Athlete*, while he was on his way to referee a Big Ten Conference basketball game. He read the magazine and began looking closely at the organization. He believed in what he found and in 1969 he started an adult chapter in Fort Dodge. Ed McNeil was a guidance counselor and coach at Fort Dodge Senior High School at the time. The insurance man talked with Ed and invited his participation. McNeil accepted and became a strong voice in advancing the FCA message. He could see almost immediately that the young men on the athletic squads in his community were benefiting from their experience with the movement. He also came to believe that the Fellowship was a positive vehicle to reach the young. From the insurance man's beginning in 1969, Ed McNeil worked with the Fellowship in Fort Dodge and, eventually, throughout the entire state of Iowa. In 1973, a board of directors was set up for a statewide office and today Ed McNeil has an FCA office in his home, where his wife works full-time for Fellowship.

McNeil played football, basketball, and baseball in high school and junior college. He played professional baseball with the Brooklyn Dodgers' farm club in Vero Beach, Florida. Today he is coach of the Fort Dodge Senior High School girls' basketball and baseball teams. But, more important to him, he continues to encourage many athletes to witness to their faith and to share their faith directly and personally with other young people and adults. He continues to lead through the Fellowship of Christian Athletes.

John Wooden, the fabled "Wizard of Westwood," who enhanced UCLA basketball fortunes with 8 national championships, represents the fine blend of care and

94

training of young athletes and devotion to his church. Wooden's honors are legion in the world of slam-dunks, driving guards, and graceful jump shots. Perhaps less known to hundreds of thousands who have watched the white-haired coach sit, arms folded, with a roll of papers in one hand, at courtside through high drama of basketball at its best, is a different kind of award. The award was given to John Wooden, churchman, for his devotion to participation in his church—the Christian Church (Disciples of Christ). It was presented at the church's international convention. Wooden has said of the Fellowship: "You'll be no saint after leaving an FCA conference, but you'll be a better person than you were."

There are the well-known to the nation—like John Wooden, Tom Landry, Tom Osborne. And some who aren't so well known, like Julian Dyke, Ed McNeil, Don Stavely, and Mike DeHesus. Mike, husband, father of 3 girls, and Vietnam veteran, was in his classroom one day in May 1976 when a representative of FCA came to see him and tell him that he had been selected as one of several coaches to attend a national conference with expenses paid. Mike was the football and wrestling coach at Warren High School in Gurnee, Illinios.

He had been thinking about a lot of things before that classroom visit, including starting a boys' "Huddle" group in his high school. But he didn't feel strong enough spiritually or physically. He had been thinking about the 37 stitches in his body as the result of being attacked by 3 hoodlums one night and his ensuing thoughts of God as he lay in the hospital recuperating. But the thoughts were just that: thoughts, not action.

Now Mike and his wife Pat thought about the conference, studied maps, and talked about which FCA site to attend. They finally settled on Denison University in Granville, Ohio.

When the DeHesus family arrived, they were im-

Coaches and players pictured in 1967 at the Blue Ridge Assembly.
Shown are (standing L to R) Ted Workman of the CFL; New York Giant
quarterback Bob Timberlake; Warrior's forward Clyde Lee; Jerry
Stovall, St. Louis Cardinal back; Chuck Walker, also of the Cardinals;

Don Shinnick of the Colts; Chicago Bear quarterback Billy Wade; (kneeling L to R) Quarterback Fran Tarkenton; Steve Sloan, Alabama Assistant Coach; Former LSU star Beau Collie; Bill Curry, Baltimore Colts; Coach Bennie Boyd.

97

mediately impressed with the beauty of the campus and the warmth and fellowship of the other coaches and their families. Before Mike DeHesus fell asleep that first night, he told his wife that he believed God had a purpose in directing them to Granville. For the first time in many, many months, the husband and wife talked privately about God. As a result of the savage attack on him that left him in a pool of blood with the side of his neck slashed open by a straight razor, Mike had already begun to reorder his life. But he still wasn't an active witness for Christ. He, Pat, and the 3 girls were deeply moved by their week's experience, however. On the final day of the conference, Mike and Pat DeHesus and their 3 daughters talked openly to each other about their feelings and needs. They acknowledged that each of them needed to accept Christ. That night a husband and a wife from Gurnee, Illinios, began a new kind of partnership. They agreed, as a result of their Fellowship experience, to begin a life of service for Christ.

Mike knew he had talents to lead young people and now he put those talents to effective use. He began the "Huddle" group that he had thought about, first with 20 young men, then with double that number. More dramatically and more courageously than starting the chapter, Mike DeHesus called his friends and his coaching associates when he and Pat returned from the week at Granville. He openly shared his experience, telling them he was reborn in Christ. He knew he would be met with looks of doubt and puzzlement, but he had found a strength in others who were actively living a Christian life. The little-known name of a high school coach in a little-known town has become a dramatic definition for the Fellowship of Christian Athletes.

Mark Julian, one of the mainstays of the Texas Tech football team that finished in the Top Ten in 1976 and was invited to the Tangerine Bowl in 1977, did some of the

Fellowship's work on the practice field in his last season on the squad. He had come to accept a verse from Colossians as a key to his life. Chapter 3, Verse 23, reads: "And whatever you do, do it heartily, as to the Lord and not unto men."

Mark approached his senior season believing he should give himself totally to the team and offer his ability with all of the enthusiasm that he possessed each day. The squad got off to a rocky start, losing a couple of close games. But he was able to shake off the disappointments and give his best, in game and in practice.

One Monday, after an especially discouraging defeat, team morale was at a low point. Mark had kept his own guideline in mind and had pushed himself as hard as he could. A teammate, with whom he had talked several times, approached him after practice. He asked Mark Julian what gave him the ability to come out to Monday practice and get going again. "Even after the kind of game we've just had," his teammate said, "you're out here giving to the glory of God and you've got a peace."

Mark sensed that his fellow player—aching physically, frustrated emotionally at the team's record to that point—was searching for something beyond a casual pep talk. Mark shared his Christian views with him and sometime later, at a Fellowship meeting, the teammate accepted Christ.

Mark Julian went on to become an assistant football coach at West Texas State University in Canyon, Texas, sharing his knowledge of the game and sharing his special gift of showing others an outline for life through which they could bring glory to God. Later he joined the FCA staff.

The dream that became the Fellowship of Christian Athletes was built, in large part, on the awareness that athletes are heroes and that heroes have a great potential for influencing others. Nowhere else on earth except perhaps in this country has the professional athlete been placed on so high a pedestal.

The Fellowship began with Doak Walker, Otto Graham, Dan Towler, and others. They proved that they weren't heroes on pedestals. They walked and talked with other men and boys about a life for Christ. It took a courage beyond the kind required to compete on an athletic field day after day, sometimes winning, sometimes losing, but always driven to excel. It took a conviction that they had a message worth the telling for a greater glory than a victory in sports. What those men started continues manyfold in the ranks of professional athletes and it continues to spread.

Marv Braden was a gifted linebacker for Southwest Missouri State University in Springfield. He was a gifted college coach at Iowa State, Southern Methodist University, and Michigan State. He is a gifted professional coach as a special teams coach for the Denver Broncos. He has been and is an eloquent and effective spokesman and worker for the Fellowship of Christian Athletes.

He remembers what the sports writers and pundits of pro ball predicted for the Broncos in their 1977 season: that Denver would finish no higher than third in their Western Division of the American Conference.

The Broncos won the division and went on to play in the Super Bowl for the first time in the team's 18-year history with an overall team record, including preseason, of 21–4. Marv remembers special reasons why much of that record was achieved. There were perhaps 16 members of the team who were in different stages of Christian commitment. Even the attitude of the non-Christians was focused on the team and not on the individual. And there wasn't, Marv Braden recalls, "any putdown, any turnoff, any negative reaction to those who had accepted a Christian life."

He remembers that some fans and television viewers

responded with skepticism when players would acknowledge thanks to the Lord after a win. But he knew that the players were sincere.

Marv Braden not only coached the special teams, he also took over the coordination of the chapel services. There was already a nucleus of committed Christians when he had arrived before the 1977 season, men like Randy Gradishar, Jack Dolbin, Steve Foley, and Phil Olsen.

In addition to the pregame chapel services, there were Bible studies on Thursday evenings and pot-luck suppers to afford the players and coaches more time with their families.

Many of the players, after their American Conference championship and their appearance in the Super Bowl, returned—along with Marv Braden—to pray for the next season. But the prayer wasn't that they would repeat as AFC winners to prove they were no flash in the pan. It was a prayer that they would maintain an attitude of humility and gratitude and never forget who was responsible for their success and the success of other men.

There are other heroes in the professional ranks who left a mark on their own kind.

It was a pregame show before a not-too-distant Super Bowl that will live in the memory of Wynn Lembright. Lembright is an ordained minister in the United Methodist Church, a regional director for the Fellowship's East-Northeast United States activities, and a former football standout at the University of Toledo. And the pregame incident, as recalled by Wynn, will live in the minds of countless young people who look up to Christian athletes: A number of the most valuable players from previous Super Bowls had been assembled for the show. The interviewer asked each to relate his most memorable moment in the game for which they had been honored. Joe Namath, of course, was among them. The dead-eyed and dead-accurate passer had been acclaimed as the Most Valuable Player in Super Bowl III, and rightly so. This was the Joe Namath who had guaranteed that his New York Jets, underdogs by two touchdowns, the team as brash as its quarterback, would beat the Baltimore Colts, a team that had lost only one game that season; the Joe Namath who boldly marched his team to that guarantee, 16-7. He moved the Jets' offense always away from Colts linebacker Mike Curtis. He picked and probed the left side, where Colts linebacker Ordell Brasse was trying to hide an injury and where he felt he could exploit linebacker Don Shinnick and halfback Lenny Lyles.

Joe Namath completed 17 of 28 passes that January afternoon in Miami; he found receivers in a crowd; he put the ball just out of Colts reach and just within finger reach of his receivers. He helped make the Super Bowl, the match between the AFL and the NFL, legitimate—something to be looked forward to and remembered from that day on.

When asked what was his most memorable moment, Namath responded: "Right after the final gun sounded and we'd won, Don Shinnick, a linebacker for the Colts, came up to me. He congratulated me and told me not to forget to thank God. And I haven't."

Don Shinnick, pressured that afternoon by Namath's sure arm and the strong legs of Jets' running backs, was true, especially in keen defeat, to his Christian way.

Yet another name symbolizes the consummate athlete who is a committed Christian. The name is Roger Staubach. He is special, as are others in the ranks of the Fellowship, because he knows he is not special. Yet the archives of athletics would say otherwise. He is linked by his exploits on the college playing field to former great names in the FCA: Doak Walker, halfback at Southern Methodist University, won the Heisman Trophy in 1948; Alan Ameche, fullback at Wisconsin University, won the Heisman Trophy in 1954; and Roger Staubach, quarterback at the United States Naval Academy, won the Heisman Trophy in 1963.

Staubach's name is in the record books and on the tips of tongues. And he seems always to be on the television screen when there is a division championship, a conference title, a Super Bowl at stake. Adulation is lavished on him by the followers of the Dallas Cowboys. Begrudging praise, sometimes even awe, is given to him by those fans who care less for the Cowboys than their own NFL favorites.

Staubach is also in the Fellowship of Christian Athletes and is a longtime worker for that movement and its mission.

And he is today's Sunday Hero who knows what tomorrow will bring. And he speaks with sensitivity and candor about the role of hero-athletes like himself. In July of 1978, before leaving for the Cowboys' training camp, Roger Staubach opened his mind, his emotions, and his spirit to the Fellowship of Christian Athletes. His thoughts, as recorded in that interview, serve today as proof that Don McClanen's belief in men like Roger Staubach was divinely placed. Staubach was asked to talk about his experience with Christians who use, abuse, or otherwise try to take advantage of name athletes. He said:

People use us to get an audience, and I think that's good as long as what is being projected is good. But some time ago I got concerned with evangelists who use me for their "warm up." "Don't say very much," they said. My role was to draw larger crowds. My testimony didn't seem that important to them.

I wasn't too pleased with that approach so I've limited myself to evangelist Bill Glass and a few others I have confidence in. I don't mind being used as far as attracting more people to an experience in which the speaker has

Detroit Piston center Kent Benson was twice president of the FCA
Fellowship group at Indiana University.

Jeff Siemon is as active off the field for FCA as he is on the field for the Vikings.

something to say that can affect lives. That's fine. But don't invite me without giving me a chance to share those things I believe deeply in.

Another problem is using name athletes who aren't Christians to attract people to a Christian function. I don't hold anything against the non-Christian athlete, but you sure shouldn't advertise them just to draw a crowd.

Staubach was asked how he ideally would like to be treated by Christians. His answer:

I want to be respected for my personal faith and the church I'm involved with. Let's not bicker over little things. Jesus Christ is the center of my life. He's my Lord and Savior. He died for my sins and that's what it's all about.

He was asked how he determined which speaking requests and endorsements to accept and which to reject. He replied:

I've had a major problem in this area. But I've made up my mind that my speaking engagements should not be just for the money. I've tried to do more for charity and Christian groups and cut down on those with a large fee.

The problem is that with five children at home I don't like to travel a lot and have to limit the number of requests I accept. Sometimes I find myself accepting those with the big fees and saying 'no' to the others, which are more important, because I can give my testimony at them.

I'm now to the point where roughly 70 percent of my appearances are for charity and the rest for the monetary reimbursement. Any endorsements I make must be with a well-established company, a product I believe in and which fits my character.

Then Staubach was asked a question that got to the heart of the hero cult, about his own life, and how he kept a perspective about himself in the face of the adulation that he and other professionals receive. He responded:

You have to realize that if you start patting yourself on the back it comes to an end. Fame comes and goes. I went through college on top but after four years in the service had to start over. How I live my life as a Christian in preparing for eternal life is what's important. This is why Christ rose from the dead. My popularity may not be as great next year or next game, and that's why my Christian life keeps everything in focus.

He was asked to comment on the Christian community's exploitation of a star when he's hot property contrasted to the quick indifference to the star when he retires or begins to falter on the field. Staubach, who has been hot property for years, replied:

That's the nature of the business. When you're on top people want the hottest name to bring in the biggest crowd for their banquet, prayer breakfast, etc. I can't begin to fill all the requests I receive, but I try to do as much as I can, realizing I won't always be on top.

So, if others want to use me when I'm on top, I'll do the best I can. I'm not saying that capitalizing on the star is right or wrong—that's just the way it is. As a Christian, I try to say, "Lord, I'm going out and doing these things for your honor and glory."

There was a final question regarding any other thoughts Staubach might have on hero worship. He replied:

Yes. I think it's good. You need someone to follow, to give you a catalyst in life. But a Christian athlete has to be

107

careful because some people think he's trying to sell his religion. When I speak to groups about my faith, I try to mention that just because my faith is in Jesus Christ doesn't mean that they have to do the same. An individual has a relationship with Christ—not with Roger Staubach.

Christ is the real example, and the hero worship is good in allowing pro athletes who are Christian the chance to point toward the Christian life and how to develop it. But after that, hero worship stops. The real hero is Jesus Christ.

Such thoughts are the mark of someone who has thought long and hard about his life, his place, and his religion. Such is the mark of greatness in Roger Staubach. Not just greatness in the pad-against-pad, muscle-against-muscle world of a professional football player in Texas Stadium, but a greatness in the man-to-man, man-to-youth world of sharing lives and making contributions. It is part of the uniform of the legions of people who are the Fellowship of Christian Athletes.

REACHING OUT

Many men have dreams. And some, like Don McClanen, hold tenaciously to those dreams until they become realities, pieces of life that take on form, then strength, and begin to grow. Because other Christian men shared the McClanen dream, it did become a slice of life and began to become strong and to grow in its worth to people.

The Fellowship's first effort to reach out to young people through the words of coaches and athletes took place in high school auditoriums in Denver, Colorado, in the winter of 1955. Dan Towler of the Rams, Robin Roberts of the Philadelphia Phillies, George Kell of the White Sox, Carl Erskine of the Dodgers, and Vernon Law of the Pirates assembled on the floors of basketball gymnasiums. Their only props were straight-back chairs and a microphone. The theme of their first talk to the hundreds of high school students looking at them from seats in the bleachers was: "Go to the church of your choice." *Sports Illustrated* commented on that first face-to-face meeting, "Sometimes the athletes got tangled up in their own words, but their sincerity won them their listeners as few polished speakers could have."

There were other small problems that were overcome in the early days, in addition to the athletes' lack of finesse as public speakers. Bob Richards was scheduled to appear at the first summer conference in 1956 to share his beliefs and to give demonstrations of the pole-vaulting style that had won him two Olympic medals. Richards was late arriving, but he was one of the star attractions and he was not to be deterred by a late arrival and the darkness. On a rocky field on the YMCA grounds, with a makeshift landing pit, in a drizzling rain, and with automobile headlights the only illumination, Richards performed for the 256 assembled athletes and coaches, soaring over the crossbar against a night-black sky. It was a picture to remember.

After the initial success of the citywide program in Denver in 1955, other sites were selected. In 1957, programs were held in Ithaca, New York; Columbus, Indiana; Lincoln, Nebraska; Augusta, Georgia; Jacksonville, Florida; and Lawrence and Manhattan, Kansas. The second national conference was attended by 339 coaches and athletes, almost 100 more than the first venture.

The following year, 1958, the Estes Park roll-call was answered by 541 people, who found that competitive athletic contests, solitary reflection, and group discussions about Christian life were a memorable combination. The word began to spread from coach to coach, coach to athlete, and young competitor to young competitor when they returned home from Estes Park.

The Fellowship took a step toward a year-around mission in 1959 when it published its first issue of *The Christian Athlete* in March. The modest 4-page magazine set forth its purpose as being a "journal to keep you informed of the many exciting aspects of the national program, to provide an opportunity for the communication of ideas and concerns relating to the Fellowship of Christian Athletes, and to present a discussion guide for the many athletic groups meeting in churches and on campuses all across the nation." It was a wise and well-received idea. Today, the magazine has grown to 32 pages and is circulated to more than 45,000 individuals.

Gary Demarest, who had learned of the Fellowship as a seminary student in Seattle, joined the FCA staff in a full-time capacity in 1959. The need for such full-time assistance became evident that summer, when a total of 624 men and boys met for the third National Conference in Estes Park and also at a second site that was added to meet the increased interest—Lake Geneva, Wisconsin.

Demarest and McClanen shared a 2-room office when they were desk-bound, which occurred rarely. Most of their time was spent trying to cover the whole of the United States, attending citywide programs, national conferences, raising funds, and working with and through churches in communities where interest had been expressed.

It became apparent to the men that a groundwork should be laid for a regional structure with regional staffing, as the interest and activity in the Fellowship grew. Demarest was to say, years later, that one of the sources of the greatest satisfaction to him was to have seen the dreams become realities and to know that the entire program had been called into being and blessed by God.

Bob Stoddard joined the full-time staff in 1960, and the citywide rallies became more and more frequent. It was at such a rally that Raymond Berry was introduced to the Fellowship. His was just one example of the way the effort had begun to capture the attention of the greats in the athletic world.

Young athletes on the steps of Lee Hall during quiet time.

The warmth of friendship at Alamosa, Colorado, 1978.

One of the memorable events during the early years was a banquet in Pittsburgh in December of 1960. On the appointed night, the latecomers found standing room only as 600 athletes, coaches, businessmen, and clergymen came together to celebrate the Fellowship's work and to rededicate themselves to its future. It was in Pittsburgh, just a few years earlier, that Don McClanen had talked with Branch Rickey and Paul Benedum about his idea of a Fellowship, and it was a fitting and stirring tribute to the men to have such a large turnout there.

The young Fellowship took an adult step when its leaders decided to have the FCA become a membership organization. The decision was made in August of 1960 and the FCA's leadership agreed that a pin and a covenant card would be the means by which future members were known. The FCA formally agreed that it would: "One, allow those who want to feel a definite identification and part of the movement to do so by applying for a 'witness pin and covenant card.' Two, extend the Christian witness through daily conversation by wearing of the pin and receive help from carrying a covenant card reminding one of his desire to accept a meaningful rule of life."

The covenant card reads: "I, [name], believe in the role of the Fellowship of Christian Athletes. As an active church member, I pledge myself to be regular in my devotional and prayer life and to use my time and talent and treasure in the service of Christ. I will wear the FCA pin and use every opportunity to tell others of the influence of Jesus Christ in my life." It was not, as so many had found out, an organization for sissies. Rather it was an organization where the courage of Christian conviction was placed out front.

Don McClanen, who had nursed his seed into bloom, had remained totally consumed by the Fellowship and its growth. But in 1961 McClanen heard another call. He felt that God had another mission for his life; perhaps, the

114

ministry. So in 1961 he resigned from the Fellowship of Christian Athletes as its father and its first executive director and he and his family moved to Richmond, Indiana. It was there that McClanen began to study with Dr. Elton Trueblood at Earlham College. Dr. Trueblood had become a friend to Don and the Fellowship during the early years of work and worry. But the ministry that involved the cleric's collar and pulpit was not to be the place for McClanen. After several months of study, he went to the Church of the Savior in Washington, where he began a ministry that the Fellowship of Christian Athletes had prepared him well to lead. It was and remains a ministry to the poor. McClanen's years of personal sacrifice and facing the realities of day-to-day economic worries were to form the bedrock for a new cause, named "Wellspring." The two McClanens labor in the vineyard today.

Bob Stoddard, already a full-time staff member, became the second president of the Fellowship in 1962, replacing the founder. There were 2 others on the national staff that year, LeRoy King and Bill Krisher. The 3 covered the country, assisting in the formation of local chapters, insuring that plans for citywide rallies and national summer conferences did not go awry. They also continued to work to bring in needed financial gifts to fund the growing activities of the Fellowship.

And there was growth. In 1963, 4 national conferences were held Henderson Harbor, New York, and Ashland, Oregon, were added to the Estes Park and Lake Geneva meeting sites.

The *Christian Athlete*, its subscription list growing, heralded the 4 conferences with the headline: "Tremendous Response, Surprises, Fun, Sweat, even Tears for over 2,000 Enrollees." The story reported:

Most of them have crew cuts, but not all of them. Most

of them have bulging muscles, but not all of them. Some of them have a direction in life, but not many of them.

All of them have a Bible, a keen interest in athletics and a sharply drawn desire to be a good Christian.

These are the participants in the Conference of the Fellowship of Christian Athletes. These are the men and boys who make up the eager, active group who are exploring new experiences in healthy exercise, both of the body and of the mind.

Sometimes you can hear a pin drop and sometimes Yankee Stadium couldn't hold all of the noise. It's a grand time and a solemn time, superbly mixed. It's a blend of eager yells of excitement and whispered words of intense prayer. . . .

Among those participants that summer in Henderson Harbor, were Paul Dietzel, then football coach at West Point; basketball's Bob Pettit of the St. Louis Hawks; Rip Engle, football coach at Penn State; Bill Peterson, football coach at Florida State; Ben Carnevale, basketball coach at the Naval Academy; and Fred Karal, wrestling coach at the Coast Guard Academy.

At Ashland, Oregon, the other new site, were Bob Richards; John Wooden, UCLA's basketball coach; Jim Owens, football coach at the University of Washington; Mike Lude, Colorado State University football coach; and Bebe Lee, athletic director at Kansas State University.

The coaches' roster at Estes Park, where it all had begun in the summer of 1956, was equally impressive: Frank Broyles, football coach at the University of Arkansas; Dave Ferriss, former Boston Red Sox pitcher; and FCA friend and helpmate Bill Krisher, the All-American from Oklahoma University.

And there were other names. Coaches, professional and college athletes. These were lineups similar to the one that was to prompt a *Nashville Banner* sportswriter, Bill

Parker, to ask a question in his column that others now had begun to ponder: "What other cause, or organization, could assemble a staff comparable to the one the athletes and coaches were treated to hear at the Fellowship of Christian Athletes' National Conference? It's a million-dollar staff. The men donate their time and efforts to the FCA movement. Many of them pay their own expenses . . . most of them are on the schedule for only a single talk, yet come for the entire conference."

The Fellowship also had a deep loss in 1963. Bob Stoddard's already-exceptional efforts to carry on the McClanen idea were cut off in mid-life by an unexpected and fatal heart attack. James Jeffrey took the baton of leadership from Bob Stoddard's administration on December 7, 1963, and the Fellowship moved into a new area of endeavor, one that remains today as the basic strength of the organization. The adult chapter program was initiated, banding together adult volunteers in communities throughout the country. The local chapters served as resource banks for the high school and college gatherings, lending adult leadership, guidance, and direction, and spreading the word about the FCA. There were now 9 people on the national staff and the first national conference was held at Black Mountain, North Carolina, providing East Coast participants with a more convenient location and one which came to parallel Estes Park in size and tradition.

In 1966 the Fellowship formalized its ministry into the high schools and colleges and universities. It was this year that the name "huddle" was formally given to the growing numbers of groups springing up among young men in high schools. And the term Fellowship was used to designate the multiplying gatherings of college athletes who met together on campuses to enrich their Christian beliefs. Among the first huddles to be recognized was the one from Sylvan High School in Atlanta, Georgia, which

117

Golf great Nancy Lopez has served tirelessly on the Board of Trustees of the FCA.

Erratum

The caption on page
It should read:
Golf great Nancy Lope
participated in FCA eve

Former Olympic gold and silver medalist in the 800 meters, Madeline Manning Jackson, relaxes at a FCA girl's Conference.

gathered shortly after it was organized to hear former Georgia football great Benny Boyd share his witness.

In 1967, the Fellowship exploded onto the national scene. On February 12, more than 11,000 people filled Kansas City's Municipal Stadium for the Fellowship's citywide rally in its headquarters city. The crowd was the largest, up to that time, to attend an FCA-sponsored event. Bobby Richardson, the former great second baseman for the New York Yankees, weight-lifter Paul Anderson, an active worker for the Fellowship, and Reverend Bob Richards shared the platform. There were a host of others: pro football players Bill Curry, Curtis McClinton, Don Shinnick, Jerry Stovall, and Coach Tom Landry; baseball professionals Jack Aker, Wayne Causey, Don Demeter, Bart Shirley, Norm Siebern, and Dave Wickersham; and college football All-Americans John Brittenum and Dave Martin. The Kansas City gathering was more than just a one-time gathering of great names. It represented the basic outreach in a community, which was to become a standard FCA endeavor. From that rally, the Fellowship's ministry moved into the Kansas City area's prisons, youth homes, juvenile institutions, hospitals, and YMCAs.

The 8 national conferences in 1967 attracted 4,700 participants and the conference in the East, at Black Mountain, boasted on its speaker's list the names of Fran Tarkenton of the New York Giants; Steve Sloan, then assistant football coach at Alabama; Beau Collie, former LSU football player; Benny Boyd, then a Florida prep school coach; Bob Timberlake, former Giant; Clyde Lee, San Francisco Warriors; Jerry Stovall, St. Louis Cardinals; Raymond Berry, ex-Colt great; Chuck Walker, Cardinals; Don Shinnick, Colts; and Bill Wade, former great quarterback for the Chicago Bears. Truly a Who's Who!

The Fellowship leaders, now increasingly confident of the acceptance of the mission, looked for ways to meet growing needs. And where there were needs it seemed that once again there was a man there to reach out a helping hand. This time it was Don Lash. Don, a former world 2-mile record-holder, owned land near Marshall, Indiana, in the western part of the state, on which he operated a boys' summer camp. In 1967 he sold the 350-acre site to the Fellowship and worked to have Lilly Endowment, Inc., of Indianapolis establish a matching fund plan for the purchase and development of the site. Huddles, Fellowships, and chapters across the country participated in the fund-raising, pledging minimal gifts of $100.00. And they used ingenious means to raise and deliver the needed funds. The huddle in a Troy, Kansas, high school ran its check to the national office in Kansas City, 82 miles away. The 21 high school boys divided each 2-mile leg of the journey. It took all day, but when they arrived, the fund was richer with the check, and the word of the FCA had been spread further than the youthful legs had run. The Oberdorfer Foundation of New Castle, Indiana, made a significant gift. When the year came to an end, the building of a National Resource Center for the Fellowship had been assured a beginning.

Julian Dyke, who had been elected to the national board of directors in 1963, was to learn first-hand to define the words, "commitment and dedication" in 1968. He had served the Fellowship in a number of capacities: on the executive committee, the National Conference committee, and the nominating committee, which allowed him to be part of the effort in naming Tom Landry to the national board. Now he was being asked to join the national staff on a full-time basis. He had been outspoken in his belief that the Fellowship needed to be bold in moving ahead with its mission and in meeting the mushrooming growth. He was now being asked to "put shoe leather" to his faith. He was still coaching in Baltimore, had security, and increased family responsibilities. Nonetheless he felt

121

pulled toward the FCA role. He was wrestling with the decision when he was told about a meeting of the small FCA staff in Kansas City. The staff had met for prayer and had decided that if there was no money for Julian Dyke to join them and insure that he could meet his family obligations, they would be willing to forgo their upcoming salaries' raises in order to make it possible for him to join them. When he heard that story, Julian sold his home, packed up his family, and drove to Kansas City in 1968 to begin a new career. In that same year attendance at the national conferences passed the 5,000 mark: 5,400 attended conferences in 9 locations.

The Fellowship inaugurated a new community program—the Weekend of Champions—in 1969 in Knoxville, Tennessee. The event, never to be held in a city that did not have an adult chapter, brought name athletes and coaches into the cities and towns to speak at churches and schools at a Friday-through-Sunday celebration. The events always closed with a rally that was open to the public. The overwhelming response in Knoxville persuaded the FCA leaders that the Weekend of Champions was an excellent way to take the movement to the grass roots. After Knoxville came Dallas, where 160 athletes and coaches convened to tell the Fellowship story and the Gospel story. Before that rally was over, the athletes had talked about their faith in churches, high schools, civic clubs, and hospitals. One coach in attendance was Moby Benedict, baseball coach at the University of Michigan. Benedict's impression was typical of many who saw the force of the Fellowship for the first time. Previously, he had been embarrassed to say that he was a Christian because he thought others would think it unmanly of him. After his participation in the Weekend of Champions in Dallas, however, he remarked that he'd like to have a team of Christian "sissies," that he'd be willing to take on anybody in the country in athletic competition, and that he knew he would come out on top.

By 1969, more than 1,000 high school huddles had been formed and nearly 8,000 people had attended 16 national conferences. In order to be better prepared for the increasing numbers at the national conferences, the FCA in 1969 instituted a college staff program. Specially selected college athletes from around the country were trained in advance of the conference sessions. They had donated a minimum of 2 to 3 weeks serving as leaders of the huddle groups at the conferences.

A smaller dream that had grown out of the large FCA dream came true in 1969. The first annual Coaches' Conference was held at Estes Park and Julian Dyke, a former coach working full-time with the FCA, took special pride because he had dreamed of such a gathering. Remembering back to his return home from his first national conference and remembering his discussions with his wife, he had envisioned a conference exclusively for coaches and their wives, where athletic knowledge could be shared and men and women could be strengthened through Christian fellowship. He could clearly see that vision now as he looked to Estes Park.

The Weekend of Champions program was conducted in 6 major cities in 1970, and the closing rally in Jacksonville, Florida, drew a record 11,750 people. A rally that same year in Fargo-Moorhead on the North Dakota-Minnesota line was telecast to 7 states and into Canada. The FCA in 1970 also began its national recognition banquet to honor coaches, athletes, and lay people for their efforts on behalf of the organization. And the Fellowship of Christian Athletes received a special kind of recognition for itself. On October 18, 1970, John Erickson, then the basketball coach at the University of Wisconsin; Rex Kern, All-American quarterback at Ohio State University; Bobby Richardson; and Jay Wilkinson, former Duke University football player gathered at the White House. The Fellowship had been invited to provide religious services for the President of the United States on that Sunday. It had been a long trip—from a small-town college campus in Wilburton, Oklahoma, to 1600 Pennsylvania Avenue, the home of Presidents—and it had taken 16 years.

James Jeffrey stepped down as the Fellowship's third president in 1971, the year that the conferences grew to 22 and attracted 8,500 participants, with Ohio, New York, South Carolina, California, Texas, and Minnesota added to the list of states where conferences were held. And the Weekend of Champions continued strong. From all over the country, more than 5,000 people came to a small town in Oklahoma, finding accommodations in high school gyms and in residents' homes for the weekend. The community was Bartlesville, and one of the organizers of the weekend was Bill Doenges, the man whose $2,200 had propelled Don McClanen on his quest. In another small community, Fort Dodge, Iowa, 79 athletes and coaches gathered together for a Weekend of Champions. And when it ended, the sharing of faith on Friday and Saturday had spurred the growth of the FCA in that town that was to eventually lead to a statewide effort.

John Erickson, former head basketball coach at Wisconsin, former general manager of the Milwaukee Bucks, one of the participants in the 1970 Sunday service at the White House, and one of the hundreds of dedicated FCA volunteers, assumed the FCA leadership in 1972. The job of organizing now became a critical one. There were 23 people on the full-time staff, 1,500 high school huddles and college Fellowships, and 200 adult chapters.

Erickson's presence and even his eye for organization were taxed in his first full year of administration. The huddles and Fellowships increased by 100 to a total of 1,600. This meant keeping eyes on 100 new locales where the high school and college athletes met with their peers. The chapters jumped to 235 in number, and 9,700 people were counted at the 17 national conferences.

The story of the grassroots work in the FCA's home city mirrored what was happening nationwide in terms of growth. Fellowship activity had been sporadic in Kansas City until 1973. Before that year, a handful of businessmen and coaches had directed an annual Spring weekend conference at William Jewell College in Liberty, Missouri; sent area athletes to national conferences; and met occasionally for fellowship. In 1973 a small core of men, Julian Dyke among them, organized the Greater Kansas City FCA Chapter. The next year they hired Ken Schmitz, a University of Illinois graduate and golfer, as their area representative. From that small but dedicated effort in 1973, the chapter has blossomed into 40 huddles, 5 Fellowships, and 11 chapters in the metropolitan area. It was this kind of growth and excitement that commanded John Erickson's attention and prompted the FCA in 1973 to expand its national board of trustees to 30 members.

About this time, in the mid-1970s, the Fellowship began to phase out one of its earlier popular efforts—the Weekend of Champions. With visibility and credibility established through these early weekend efforts and the associated appearances throughout the country of the well-known athletes, there was less need for the 2-day gathering. In its place, many communities began to hold a Day of Champions, with a format similar to the Weekend, but limited to a single day to ease travel arrangements and to spread the Fellowship's work more evenly into other endeavors. In addition, clinics, weekend retreats, miniconferences, banquets, and one-day training sessions began emerging as events that athletes, coaches, and business and community leaders wanted to attend.

The National Resource Center was ready for programs in 1974 and the FCA promptly shifted into a new and receptive field: the female athlete and coach. The first women's conferences were held at the Indiana site in 1974

126

and the response provided a clear direction for the Fellowship to follow in serving the growing number of female competitors and coaches. FCA's board of trustees did not wait for the first foot to be firmly planted in the world of female athletics before it took its second step: the huddle and Fellowship concept of organizing groups on high school and college campuses was expanded to include senior high school and college women. The board also agreed to encourage junior high school huddles.

There were 28 national conferences held in 1974 and the FCA counted some 10,000 names on the lists of people who attended. The full-time staff numbered 78 people as the planning and organizational efforts required the efforts of more and more people.

In 1975, Tom Landry found himself a long way from the sideline stripe in Texas Stadium. He stood in front of a microphone in Marshall, Indiana, where he assisted, along with the governor of the State of Indiana, Otis R. Bowen, in the formal dedication of the National Resource Center. The leader of a state and the leader of a world-champion football team were appropriate choices to help launch the center. The facility, carefully laid out to make full use of its 350 acres, had accommodations for 150 people, a lake with a swimming area, an open-air pavilion covering 4 full-size basketball courts, a 4-court tennis complex, 22 acres of athletic fields, and the 255-seat Kresge Chapel. The date was June 1, 1975. By the middle of August 1975, the Center had hosted 10 of that year's 28 national conferences. Four weeks set aside for high school girls brought such an enthusiastic response from the participants that a fifth week was added in that year.

The Reverend Dick Armstrong's prayer of dedication for the Center was dramatically answered during the first weeks of operation after the ceremonies. He had said, "We pray that those who come here to enjoy the excitement of athletics and the beauty of this setting may dis-

128

cover the joy of Christian fellowship . . . and the centrality of Jesus Christ for their lives."

Those who came for the enjoyment and thrill of athletics found plenty to get excited about. The first basketball camp was directed by Dick Harp, former Kansas University coach and executive vice-president of FCA; Dean Smith, coach at the University of North Carolina; Walt Shublom of Kansas City Community College; Tex Winter of Northwestern; Guy Strong of Oklahoma State; Gordon Stauffer of Indiana–Purdue University at Fort Wayne; and John Erickson, former coach and FCA president. An impressive array of coaching talent!

And those who came for athletic excitement also found something deeper and more lasting. During one week at the National Resource Center, 70 delegates were on hand. Of those, 26 indicated that they had found Christ as Savior and Lord, 29 made recommitments of their lives, and 22 said they would like to become more involved in full-time Christian service. The center was one of the Fellowship's tangible resources, but it also began to serve immediately as a resource for Christ and His church.

The emphasis continued in 1976 on a ministry to serve women. The emphasis on women's sports was one of the great changes in the 1970s and the FCA reflected this increased awareness. In the summer of 1976, a women's program director was added to the full-time staff and the first girls' national conference was held at Oral Roberts University in Tulsa, Oklahoma.

In order to supplement the role of *The Christian Athlete* magazine, the Fellowship decided in 1976 to publish a national newsletter to keep its membership advised of work on behalf of the FCA and the church being done by huddles, Fellowships, and chapters throughout the United States. The newsletter, published 6 times a year, was aptly named *The Widening Circle.*

The FCA also designated 6 official regions in the country in order to provide quicker and more effective staff aid to the groundswell of interest: Philadelphia, Atlanta, Indianapolis, Dallas, Denver, and San Francisco.

The Kresge Chapel, which had its origin in the generosity of Stanley and Dorothy Kresge of Detroit, Michigan, was officially dedicated during the annual fall meeting of the national staff on Sunday, October 10, 1976.

There was one setback in an otherwise banner year. On Sunday, November 28, 1976, 6 weeks after Kresge Chapel had been dedicated, a fire destroyed the Benedum staff lodger adjacent to the chapel. Fortunately, there were no injuries and the chapel was not harmed. Out of the ashes would come 4 new structures, each to house 12 persons.

The Fellowship was assured of a place in the national life of the country's Christian athletes by 1977, and that year marked more, and perhaps more difficult, decisions to face.

There was a pressing need for larger quarters for the national staff. On April 21, 1977, the board of trustees faced that need and made its decision. The board committed the course of the Fellowship to a National Headquarters Building and a chapel adjacent to the Harry S. Truman Sports Complex in Kansas City. The building would be on a 1.8-acre site overlooking the Kansas Royals Stadium. It would consist of 25,000 square feet spread over 3 floors. More important, it would cost $1.6 million, a figure that was nearly one thousand times the amount that Bill Deonges, the automobile dealer in Bartlesville, Oklahoma, had provided to Don McClanen in 1954.

But the Fellowship had friends who believed in its mission, people to extend a hand of assistance and help. The Mabee Foundation of Tulsa, Oklahoma, was made up of such believers and committed itself to an $800,000 challenge grant, requiring that the rest of the funding be committed before December 31, 1977. The Fellowship was about to find out just how deeply the belief in its ministry went. It knew it had to rely on contributions, grants, and gifts of all sizes. Coach Landry, then the immediate past president of the FCA, perhaps best summed up the depth of that belief. He said, when the board made the decision in 1976 to seek a Kansas City site: "God has given us a vehicle in the Fellowship to convey the message of faith through the common denominator of sports. We believe that a National Headquarters Building will allow us to minister in an even broader scope, releasing funds now used in office rental."

With the decision made on the national headquarters, the leadership of the Fellowship now turned its attention to even more complicated decisions. After 23 years of growth, it was time to look anew at the FCA's purpose.

Out of a 4-day meeting of the 23 officers and directors of the Fellowship in August 1977 came these tenets that would provide a consistency to the FCA's policies and practices:

The overall purpose of the Fellowship of Christian Athletes was modified to read, "A movement to present to athletes and coaches, and all whom they influence, the challenge and adventure of receiving Jesus Christ as Savior and Lord, serving Him in their relationships and in the fellowship of the church."

This purpose was affirmed with renewed emphasis on the church. A lower case "c" was used to denote a person's local church. A capital "C" was used to refer to all Christians throughout the world. A renewed emphasis was also placed on the coach.

The statement of purpose continued: "The FCA model can be best implemented when coaches are involved in some type of a sponsor or supportive role resulting in coaches and athletes participating in their local church. Thus an evaluation of the FCA's ministry could be the degree of local church involvement by those it serves."

131

The officers and directors went further. They set forth new purposes and new definitions to the expanded areas of the ministry.

The purpose of the huddles and Fellowships was "to provide an environment for developing fellowship, personal Christian growth, service opportunities, and involvement with the church."

Because the foundation of the Fellowship was the athlete, a definition of "athlete" was included: "Eligible participants for junior high and senior high huddles are to be members of recognized school athletic teams. Eligible participants for the Fellowships on college and university campuses are to be past or present members of recognized school athletic teams."

Lastly and perhaps most importantly, because of the crucial role of a coach in the growth and development of young people, there was a section addressed to coaches: "Realizing the significant ministry coaches can have with their athletes, FCA's intention is to make the coaches' ministry a priority consideration with emphasis on providing an environment for developing fellowship, personal Christian growth, and an opportunity for involvement and leadership in FCA's ministry."

The discussions by the officers and board, long and sometimes labored, came at a propitious time. The Fellowship of Christian Athletes in 1977 had grown to 2,000 huddles and Fellowships and 300 chapters. In that year, 8 National Resource Center weeks were held, 3 national conferences for women were conducted, and 3 coaches' conferences were held.

The women's conferences were of particular pride to the FCA staff. Cindy Smith, Director of Girls' Programs, found an overwhelming response from volunteers in the ranks of women coaches and other women adults. The conferences in 1977 were held at the site of the first women's conference—Oral Roberts University—and at

132

Colorado State University in Fort Collins, Colorado, and Lees-McRae College in Banner Elk, North Carolina. The Fort Collins gathering was symbolic of the 3 conferences. More than 475 girls attended and, near the end of their time together, as a rainbow suddenly added beauty and drama to the setting, one group of girls summed up their experience: "With every tear and smile we moved a little closer to God—and we had a lot of both this week."

The year 1977 also marked the beginning of a new ministry, one that had had its beginning in 1964 aboard a navy ship sailing with the 6th Fleet somewhere in the Mediterranean.

Bill Lewis, a naval officer, had met Bob Davies, a former NBA Hall of Famer, when Lewis was stationed in Mechanicsburg, Pennsylvania, and Davies was a Sunday school teacher in nearby Gettysburg. Shortly after the two became friends, Bill Lewis received orders to report aboard a 6th Fleet ship. Mail call one day in 1964 aboard ship somewhere in the Mediterranean brought to Lewis a note from Davies and a copy of The Christian Athlete magazine. The note suggested that Lewis "might like this outfit." Lewis read the magazine, was impressed with what he read, and began to correspond and send a little money to the FCA headquarters. It was a relationship, known all too well to men aboard ships, that began and grew on paper.

Lewis's next assignment, in 1966, was at the Pentagon. He became involved in FCA efforts in the Washington area. He helped start the Greater Washington, D.C., chapter with the help of Otto Graham, then coach of the Redskins.

In 1968 Lewis felt a growing conviction that God was calling him to accept a full-time position with the FCA, now a very large part of his life. He took early retirement from the Navy and became the Mid-Atlantic Regional Director for the Fellowship. His retirement as a Captain in the Navy and his signing on with the FCA meant going home again to a place where he had lived and worked and grown as a person and as a naval officer. He settled in Annapolis, Maryland, site of the United States Naval Academy. During his years as a midshipman, he had been the No. 1 golf and No. 1 squash player for the Academy.

While in the Washington-Baltimore area, Bill Lewis served for 8 years as the lay chaplain for the Baltimore Colts. And, demonstrating that the Fellowship of Christian Athletes plays no favorites, he also helped Otto Graham begin a spiritual effort with the Washington Redskins. What had started as an exchange of letters from aboard ship in 1964 was to take Bill away from the green playing fields of football stadiums and back to the green stretches of golf courses. He persuaded the FCA board to let him lead the effort to establish a golf ministry.

On October 1, 1977, Lewis became the national director of FCA's golf ministry. Its purpose was to challenge golfers and coaches, male and female, to follow Jesus Christ as Savior and Lord in the fellowship of the church.

This new arm of the FCA started cautiously, testing its muscle. It began with Golf Days of Champions featuring junior high and high school tournaments, first locally and statewide. Local golf professionals, college coaches, and college golfers would act as big brothers to the younger players. Each would start with a morning devotional to be followed by instruction and competition. The response was good. Bill Lewis set his sights on a program tournament for the following year. The new arm proved to have strong muscle.

On October 3, 1977—a Monday evening—in the Kansas City Chiefs' Arrowhead Stadium, the Fellowship received a special blessing. Lamar Hunt, owner of the Kansas City Chiefs, in a ceremony prior to the kickoff of the Monday night game between the Chiefs and Oakland Raiders, presented a check to FCA President John Erickson. The check, from the National Football League Charities, was a grant to assist in the construction of the FCA's proposed headquarters and chapel. Hunt was a member of the NFL Charities Board of Directors and the FCA's National Board of Trustees. The check was for $20,000. It was a rewarding way in which to wind down another year in the ministry of the Fellowship.

The numbers continued to swell in 1978. More than 15,000 coaches attended the 4 national coaches' conferences, clinics, breakfasts, and other gatherings. The staff was now at more than 100 full-time employees; and 32 national conferences were held during the summer. For the first time, a national girls' conference was held in each of the Fellowship's 6 regions.

And just as Don McClanen had maintained a rock-strong faith in his dream, a latter-day dream of the FCA began to take form. On February 11, 1978, John Erickson stood in a long line with several other people who had a special interest in and a special love for the Fellowship. They wore construction hard-hats and they held shovels. At a signal, they drove the shovels into a mound of dirt snaking in front of the line and tossed it into the air. Ground was broken for the new National Headquarters Building and Chapel.

The National Resource Center in Marshall, Indiana, was being used to capacity and beyond in 1978. The center's director, Charles Miller, and his wife Lib, had become known to thousands of young people who had found their own personal rewards and moving experiences under the direction of the Millers. The Fellowship purchased an additional 100 acres adjacent to the Marshall site and decided, in another bold step, in late 1978, to launch a major fund drive to expand the center's capacity to 250 participants. It was a year short of the 25th anniversary of the Fellowship of Christian Athletes—a year in which tens of thousands of men, women, boys, and girls could look with pride and thanks at being part of a movement truly sharing the victory given by God through Jesus Christ.

TODAY

On May 21, 1979, Don McClanen went home again, a trip that encompassed dreams and time as well as miles. He traveled to Kansas City, Missouri, to stand on a podium before a microphone and 1,200 people. Don took his turn, along with others, at putting thoughts into words. The day was the day of dedication for the FCA's National Headquarters Building. The backdrop for Don McClanen was the centerpiece for the day—the building, gleaming in the bright Kansas City sun and rising 3 stories behind him with sharp modern architectural angles. The statistics of the building were impressive: 1.8 acres of land, 25,000 square feet of floor space, steel-frame and precast-concrete construction, bronze-tinted insulating glass, ramps and elevators for the handicapped, and a cost of $1.6 million.

More impressive than the statistics of the building was

the way in which the money had been raised. The Mabee Foundation's $800,000 challenge had started it all and more than $700,000 came from the Kansas City business and professional community. In all, more than 500 individuals, businesses, and foundations throughout United States contributed. The amounts ranged from a single dollar to the $800,000 from Mabee. It had been a dramatic example of sharing a victory. When the fund drive ended, the Fellowship had raised $2.5 million. After the building was paid for, the remaining money was placed in a trust fund for the building's operating expenses.

John Erickson breathed a sigh of relief. He had seen the FCA through unexpected and unparalleled growth, sometimes almost too rapid to handle. He had guided the Fellowship through uncertain financial times as needs pressed hard against an always modest checkbook. He was surrounded, on that day in May, with success and with the old and the new friends of the Fellowship who had come to dedicate the building and share in the jubilation. Erickson turned briefly to the past: "We have endured," he said, "despite periods of national and international upheaval, as well as major changes in the world of athletics. So long as we're faithful to our mission of sharing the victory, I believe that we will continue to have a viable and meaningful ministry."

Then he shifted to the present: "We will actively continue our goal of reaching every high school, junior high, college, and pro athlete with our program. And while we have touched many, our goal also is to encourage those who have declared their faith, to live their faith."

The Fellowship does encourage and acknowledge people. Also on the night of May 21, 1979, more than 1,000 people filed into the banquet room of the Crown Center Hotel in Kansas City. For the 10th consecutive year, the FCA honored people for their FCA activity, athletic achievement, and church and community involvement. The gathering was the 10th annual National Recognition Banquet of the Fellowship. Many of those who had attended the dedication of the headquarters earlier in the day were at the hotel that night as John Erickson emceed the occasion.

The people honored that night are examples of why and how the FCA reaches out:

• A young man from Terre Haute, Indiana, received the Bob Stoddard Memorial Award. The young man, Malcolm "Cam" Cameron, had read Scripture in front of the dedication crowd that morning. That night he was honored as an All-State quarterback at South High School in Terre Haute, as a member of the Academic All-American team, and as one of the founders of the first FCA huddle in southern Indiana.

• Joyce Gibson, a student-athlete at South Tama High School, Iowa, was named winner of the Gladys Kelce Award. Joyce was a leading scorer on the basketball squad, a competitor in cross-country, softball, and track, and she was president of the honor society and girls' huddle at her school.

• Scott Hall, 6 feet, 2 inches, 185 pounds, and a senior at Wheaton College in Illinois, was chosen to receive the FCA's College Athlete Award. Scott had been named to an All-American team as a quarterback and had compiled a career completion record of 374 passes for 4,489 yards. He had served 4 years on the FCA's college staff and had spoken frequently for the Fellowship in the Chicago area.

• Cindy Andrews, a University of Arizona senior and standout volleyball player, was the female recipient of the College Athlete Award. She had led the Sun Devils to the NCAA volleyball tourney 2 out of 3 years and she guided the women's Fellowship on her campus for 3 years.

• Brooks Robinson, revered Baltimore Orioles third baseman, was named by the FCA as its Pro Athlete Award winner. Robinson's career with the Orioles from 1955 to

Roger Staubach, the All-American at the Naval Academy and the veteran quarterback of the Dallas Cowboys.

Roger Staubach, speaking at a
Weekend of Champions in 1971.

Bobby Jones of the Philadelphia
76ers is an active FCA member.

Veteran Major League first baseman Andre Thornton, an active FCA
member, putting the tag on Jim Rice.

1977 brought him nearly every honor in baseball. He played in 18 All-Star Games and won the Golden Glove Award for 12 consecutive years.

• Tom Landry was named winner of the FCA's 1979 Coaching Award. He had been a stalwart of the FCA since being introduced to the movement in 1962. His coaching career with the Dallas Cowboys included 13 consecutive winning seasons and 5 Super Bowl appearances.

Along with the athletes and the coaches were lay persons who were honored. There was Donald Moyers, a Tulsa lawyer, civic leader, and friend of the Fellowship; he was a Life Trustee of the FCA and a person instrumental in securing the Mabee grant for the construction of FCA's new headquarters. Also honored was Gladys Kelce, a former school teacher who made the FCA's Women's Program a reality in 1976 when she gave a gift for that purpose. Dr. Roe H. Johnston of LaGrange, Illinois, was one of the FCA's founders and tireless early workers.

These lives were touched by the Fellowship in a special way in Kansas City on the night of May 21, 1979, but more than 10,000 lives were touched throughout the country at the conferences that summer. The FCA could count 150 Huddles in the nation's junior high schools, 1,300 huddles in senior high schools, and 200 Fellowships on college and university campuses. There were 31 conferences held from coast to coast in 1979, including 6 for coaches and 5 for high school and college girls.

The dedication had been moving for Don McClanen and the men who had walked with him in the early years. Dan Towler and Dr. Louis Evans, Sr., were in Kansas City to lead in thanksgiving for the success of the FCA. They could look back and remember the dream, the need for money, the first handful of committed athletes, the small offices, the young and inexperienced staff trying to cover a nation, the debts, the loans, the gifts, and then the debts again.

Now there was a $1.6-million building to accommodate 40 of FCA's 130 employees. There was a modern film series titled "The Athletes." Already 17 such films had been produced by the Southern Baptist Radio and Television Commission, each a 14-minute color feature on FCA personalities like Grant Teaff, Don Kessinger, Mel Kenyon, Tommy Bell, Tom Landry, and Bunny Martin.

There was a golf ministry that had grown from modest tournament play and instruction·for high school players to a national Pro-Am in September 1979 in Fairfax, Virginia. Larry Nelson, winner of the Gleason in March 1979, and Andy Bean, No. 3 money-winner in 1978, were among the top names. Others were Tommy Aaron, Curtis Strange, Orville Moody, Lee Elder. There were more than 40 nationally known pros. Bill Lewis's idea had taken hold and had been helped by individuals and organizations interested in the FCA and in golf. The First Annual FCA Pro-Am was sponsored by one of the larger banking networks in Virginia, First and Merchants Bank. The Country Club of Fairfax donated its golf course and facilities for the event.

But more important than the bricks and the steel, than the organization and its extensions, are the men and women, the boys and girls whose lives have been touched by the ministry. In its 25th year, the Fellowship of Christian Athletes can look back on its past and know that it has helped thousands and thousands move to a stronger Christian life.

Year after year, the letters of praise and thanks arrive at FCA headquarters. Many recount personal experiences at national conferences. One letter perhaps best sums up the meaning of the national conference. It is from Noreen Whitworth, the mother of a young participant. She wrote it after he returned to their South Pasadena, California, home. She said:

Geoff Zahn, pitching ace of the Minnesota Twins and active FCA member.

Former Chicago White Sox player-manager Don Kessinger has been active in FCA for many years.

He was a quiet kid . . . a good athlete and a good student. He was 16 and introspective. There were a lot of maybes, a lot of questioning; the usual amount of doubt about values, human relationships, society's hangups, personal acceptance. The where am I going? . . . whose beat do I step to? . . . what am I? . . . what do I really believe? . . . where is it at? . . . all those seekings, searchings that the youth of our day must face. He was going to an FCA national conference. The kids in his family rarely had gone to a camp of any kind.

What was the FCA?

That initial answer: a bunch of Christian guys, athletically oriented. There are coaches and athletes from all facets of sports. They talk with the kids, conduct clinics. And they give you a Bible.

Okay. Sounds good . . . so long, son, enjoy yourself.

The days pass rapidly . . . it's Friday. He's back. How'd it go? Still looks the same . . . a little tanner . . . and 10 pounds heavier (the food was terrific). But he's grown, inside . . . somehow it's all come together. He's smiling and confident in his outlook. He talks about the great time, the guys, the men he's met, the people he's lived with . . . the God who's real . . . the values that count . . . his values . . . his direction . . . his belief . . . his astonishing discovery . . . himself. "It's great to be me. I can contribute; I do owe my brother a lot. My parents are human, too, and they love and make mistakes, but they try and they're mine,"

A guy gives 100 percent of himself all the time but it's relative. There's meaning. To borrow a phrase, "that's where it's at" . . . FCA . . . no flowery approach this . . . just gutsy stuff in terms he understands. And it's not a passing phase . . . it's a dedication and a direction. This attitude endures, is firm and real. He has a point of reference . . . The Book is read . . . it too sustains, it too is relevant.

As a parent, I have said, "I'd scrub floors to give my

other sons the opportunity to be part of an FCA experience" ... what parent wouldn't?

A kid of 16 went to an FCA conference; a confident, Christian young man returned.

The Fellowship of Christian Athletes continues to reach out and touch hearts and spirits, and it seems assured of continued success. There are people like Don Shinnick, who met the Fellowship in its early days, to worry about growth and dependence on the Lord. He started a Huddle in the Amador Valley of California before moving to a new coaching job in Fayette, Missouri, at Central Methodist College.

"Pogo" Smith plans to stay on as an advisor to Fellowships like the one at Vanderbilt, as long as the students ask. He continues to find joy in the national conferences, where his daughter is in charge of the teenage girls. He believes that the FCA's future is assured because, "Through the years and its great growth, it has consistently supported the church. While some other organizations have, from time to time, been a little critical of the church, the FCA never has."

Ed McNeil, spending a lifetime being close to and caring about young athletes, believes that the Fellowship's mission is more vital today than ever before: "I think we've just scratched the surface. The need is becoming more and more apparent because of the problems creeping into our society. More and more coaches are going to want to become involved and get their young people involved."

Dan Stavely guards against a future for the FCA without continued emphasis on the coach: "The success of a Fellowship program, high school or college, boy or girl, is the leadership that's involved. You've got to have a coach. And he's got to be interested and the kids have to know that he's interested.

147

Heisman Award winner Archie Griffin, now

with the Bengals, is a staunch supporter of FCA.

"He's able to motivate these young people and relate to them in a way that's unique. The player-coach relationship cannot be replaced by any other. There's a special bond that exists between the coach and the people he works with. And the FCA needs to provide whatever resources it can to help the new young coaches feel comfortable in being Christian leaders."

Gary Demarest, who has a view of the Fellowship from its infancy to its 25th year, insures its vitality by stressing the importance of the layperson. "My dream would be that in every major geographical region of the United States that we'll have a staff and a whole group of volunteers doing FCA work with and through the churches, reaching out to boys and girls in athletics and helping them to share the same kind of Christian fellowship that so many of us have experienced."

Richard Armstrong, who also spans the efforts of the Fellowship from its beginning to its present, enhances the present by recalling the past. He notes: "There have been moments of agony as well as joy, many laughs and not a few tears, all of which serve to strengthen our oneness in Christ and remind us that this movement of which we are a part belongs to God and not to us. As long as we are faithful to Him and depend on His grace, we can trust our next quarter century will be even brighter than the first."

Don McClanen, the dreamer whose dream became the Fellowship of Christian Athletes, offers words to affirm the future of the Fellowship as well as any other person. On that day in May, as he stood before the assembled crowd to help dedicate a building, he said:

May we commence our invocation by first hearing God's word. It seems so very appropriate in the 127th Psalm. 'If the Lord does not build the house, the work of the builders is useless; if the Lord does not protect the city, it does no good for the sentries to stand guard. It is useless to work so hard for a living, getting up early and going to bed late. For the Lord provides for those He loves, while they are asleep.'

Our Father, we pause at the beginning of this dedication service to praise and thank You for the 25-year history that seems, somehow, to be symbolized in the concreteness, in the bricks and mortar, in the beauty of this new headquarters building. While rejoicing in this accomplishment given by Your provision, we would remind ourselves that it is in the building of dignified human lives that You take up residence and make them temples of Your Holy Spirit.

So on this special day of celebration, we would ask that You breathe the vital breath of Your Spirit on this structure. That both the persons who enter this place for work and mission as well as the very building itself will serve as a life-transforming movement and monument to Your glory.

Come to us now in this day and hour, O Lord, that You have created and given to us in such beauty. Come to us with Your majesty and transforming power. As a result, may the youth of this nation and the athletic arena of this world be reborn and reshaped from within, the Kingdom of Your holy will. We love You, we worship You, we adore You. In Christ's precious name we pray. Amen.

...AND
TOMORROW

The phone rang in the office of the head basketball coach at the University of Wisconsin and coach John Erickson answered it. An old friend, Frank McGuire, was calling. McGuire was head basketball coach at the University of North Carolina and he needed Erickson's assistance.

McGuire explained that he was actually calling for a friend of his, Ben Carnevele, who was head basketball coach at the Naval Academy.

Carnevele and McGuire were to participate at a basketball clinic at Lake Geneva, Wisconsin, about 50 miles from Erickson's campus in Madison. McGuire said he wanted to borrow some basketballs and some scrimmage shirts.

Erickson responded that he'd be happy to oblige. Before he put the phone back in the cradle, he asked, "Frank; what did you say the name of the outfit is that's sponsoring the clinic?"

153

"The Fellowship of Christian Athletes," McGuire answered.

"Well, I've never heard of it. But I'll meet you down there and we'll talk some basketball," Erickson said.

The need for basketballs and scrimmage shirts at a 1959 clinic was to change the course of John Erickson's life. Erickson loaded the balls and the shirts into his car and drove to Lake Geneva for the clinic. While there, he became interested in the Fellowship of Christian Athletes. Upon returning to his home and to his job at the University of Wisconsin, John Erickson began to realize that he didn't have the confidence about his life's purpose that others at the clinic did. He finally acknowledged to himself that he should be working and coaching for a purpose other than self-centeredness. That realization spurred him to recommit his life to Christ. He had been a strong churchman, but he had no personal relationship, and so he committed his life and his coaching to Christ. It was the result of a single FCA clinic and the people he had met there.

He began working as a volunteer for the FCA. He attended national conferences, taking carloads of youngsters with him; he spoke at gatherings for the Fellowship and worked to enlarge its horizons.

Erickson's contributions of labor and time to the FCA continued until 1968, when he began a new career. He joined the Milwaukee Bucks basketball organization as general manager and vice-president. Suddenly the summers were busy with work for the upcoming seasons and the national conferences had to be put aside. John Erickson continued, however, to speak and to work for the Fellowship whenever he could.

By 1972 John had left the Bucks, run once for the United States Senate, and was the vice-president of a large construction concern in Wisconsin. He received a call one day from Dick Armstrong, vice-president of Princeton

Theological Seminary, an FCA board member, and a member of Tom Landry's Search Committee to find a replacement for James Jeffrey, who had stepped down as the FCA's president. Dick Armstrong wanted to talk about a new leader for the FCA. The talk was inconclusive, but Armstrong was persistent in his interest in talking to John. In August 1972, he was in Milwaukee for a Presbyterian church retreat and he stayed with the Ericksons. Again he talked about the needs of FCA leadership.

The next call that John Erickson answered was from Tom Landry. The coach of the Cowboys wanted John to come to Dallas for a meeting of the search committee. John sensed the committee might be looking to him to take on the job. He told Landry that he would help find the right person, but that he wasn't interested.

John's premonition about the job grew on his way to Dallas. His plane schedule had been modified by the FCA. He had to first fly into Los Angeles to meet with Donn Moomaw, a member of the search committee who couldn't attend the Dallas meeting.

When John finally arrived in Dallas shortly after Labor Day, he had made up his mind that if the job were offered to him, he would decline. He had plans for another try at politics, and his present obligations to his family and firm simply wouldn't allow him to make such a move.

But Tom Landry was insistent. After the committee had met, Landry met with Erickson.

"John, the committee would like to extend an invitation to you to take the position." Landry fixed his eyes on John's eyes in a way that only Landry can do. John Erickson was to remember those eyes and that look years later. Erickson was deeply moved at the confidence this caliber of men had expressed in him, but he didn't want the job. He asked for some time to think, promising to get back to Landry no later than early November.

John Erickson went home and looked for, almost hoped

John Erickson, current FCA President

Ron Morris, V.P. of Special Projects.

John Erickson shows his form with a shovel at the ground-breaking ceremony, February 1978.

The headquarters building beginning to take shape in the fall of 1978.

The culmination of a dream comes with the dedication of completed headquarters, May 21st, 1979.

for, obstacles to taking the job. But when Tom Landry and Alicia Landry came to Milwaukee for a Cowboys' game against the Green Bay Packers, John told Tom, "Yes, I'll do it. I'll be there by November 15. But I want a commitment from you that you'll give me 3 years as chairman of the FCA board."

Landry agreed. He served a 3-year term as chairman, went off the board, and came back on.

John Erickson remains as president of the Fellowship. The confidence that was placed in him by Tom Landry and others on that 1972 Search Committee has been rewarded. And it will continue to be rewarded as John Erickson looks at the future of the Fellowship of Christian Athletes.

Erickson believes the FCA today knows well what its future mission will be. He notes: "We will remain true to the original purpose. We will continue to serve the Gospel, not to try to manage it. The leadership of the FCA will continue to try to discern what God has in mind for the Fellowship."

There have been some changes, however. Erickson feels one of the greatest has been in the composition of the FCA at the grass roots. "We don't know how long coaches and athletes will continue to have the platform that they have now. In 1954, for example, they didn't have nearly the platform they do today. The ministry then was almost solely involved with professionals. Today the largest segment is the high school, junior high school, and collegiate area, both men and women. While we try to minister to the pros, we probably don't have as many pros involved with the Fellowship in this period of time."

But, inevitably, John Erickson and others in the Fellowship come back to the mission, as it began under Don McClanen and as it remains today. "Even if sports were to disappear in the future, the mission of the Fellowship wouldn't. We will continue to present the Gospel. I don't think God would speak to us and say that the Fellowship of Christian Athletes isn't needed anymore. Rather I think He would say that something else is needed. Much in the future will depend upon what God has in mind for us."

Erickson believes that the Fellowship will always go where coaches and participants are. He points out the near-explosion in participation sports that were almost nonexistent 25 years ago. Swimming, tennis, golf, even jogging are areas of interest to the FCA, John notes. He points to the 800 FCA members who are rodeo riders. He talks about the rapidly growing golf ministry. He tells of the interest in the FCA by race-car drivers. All of these he sees as signs that the Fellowship is ministering to more than simply yesterday's well-known football, basketball, and baseball participants.

But Erickson doesn't believe in growth for the sake of growth. The FCA, he feels, is not interested in the numbers game.

"We did have a period of exceptional growth beginning in 1964. In that year the Fellowship began to serve the Huddles, chapters, and Fellowships. We became, in a real sense, a daily ministry. Before that, we had concentrated in large measure on the national conferences. But in 1964 we began to be an organization that responded to daily needs in the communities." Erickson points out that that was a case of adhering to the purpose of serving God, not simply trying to enlarge membership rolls.

The Fellowship has grown into a truly national ministry since its founding. With local chapters spread across the land, John Erickson feels that the FCA can and will respond to any part of the country where there is a need or a desire for the Fellowship's work.

But a national ministry takes money, and Erickson sees the years ahead as a time in which the FCA must work to become self-sufficient. "We need to remove the burden from the contributors, who give sacrificially, and develop

Veteran Dolphin linebacker Tim Foley during "Quiet Time."

perhaps a national endowment. We now have a coordinated budget plan for the entire ministry. But we need a way to allow all contributions to be fed directly into the veins of the Fellowship, used solely to send youngsters to conferences, coaches to clinics, and families to retreats and Bible studies. In the future we will need sources of income other than those that we have now."

In the fall of 1979, John Erickson, fourth president of the Fellowship of Christian Athletes, stated with deep conviction and humility:

From the innermost parts of my being, I would pray for those who have been involved in this ministry.

I think that in the first 25 years we have had many coaches and athletes profess Jesus Christ and His ways, and the word of God. They have been people who very much would like to live the alternative lifestyle that the Scriptures would provide for us.

I think that we have all found it extremely difficult in the first 25 years of the Fellowship to be the kind of models to the world that we'd really like to be in living out the Gospel.

It would be my hope that in the years ahead those athletes and coaches who truly profess Christ and His Gospel will begin to truly live the Gospel in such a way in our sports activities, in our relationships one with another in life, that it truly will help alter the world in which we live.